GAMEPLAN
WORKBOOK

The Complete Strategy Guide
to go from
Starter Kit to Silver

Sarah Harnisch
Young Living Platinum

Contents

APPENDIX

The Gameplan Comprehensive Strategy Workbook

HOW TO USE THIS BOOK

This workbook is written for both those both brand new to Young Living as well as those who have been working the business for a while. How can it be helpful for both? Let me explain.

To the brand new business builders...

This is a tool to help you see your business plan clearly and set tangible goals. It's for those of you who need to pour over the words in Gameplan and write them out to get them cemented in your minds. Walk the paths of hope with me throughout this workbook. Put it all on paper. Take a look inside your notes every six months and see how close you have gotten to attaining the rank of your dreams. It works! If you speak life over your dreams, it's amazing what starts to happen.

A woman once told me she didn't feel right praying for large things. She said that there were people starving all over the world, and it was immoral to pray for such a large income.

Hear my heart, weary mom, weary dad, and overworked worker: the desires of your heart are not yours. They were planted there by a much bigger God—One who has dreams for you that you can't even fathom. So chase the dreams. Put feet to your hopes. Dare to put them on paper, pray them aloud, and put one foot in front of another as you get closer and closer to the vision you see for your life, to the vision that was laid out over you before you were even born. You have permission to dream large. And you have permission to get there.

How can you help the widows, the poor and the sick when the head gasket is out in your car and you are short for your student loan payments this month? You can't pour into others when you are drowning. I believe with all my heart that the Lord wants abundance for His children. We just never claim it. We never believe it. And so it passes us by.

Never again. Your period of poverty is over. The famine has ended. And it's time to make some changes. It's time to have a Gameplan.

It's time to hit the goals you have thought about for years, but never actually ran toward. This is your book, dreamer. Let's lay out some plans together, side by side. I am the momma that had nothing—spent 36 years in poverty—and went from starter kit to Platinum in 17 months with no friend circle and no time. If I can do it, you can do it. It takes rolling up your sleeves, planning where you are going, and what you are moving toward. This book is your plan. You will be blown away at what the Lord does as you speak this aloud, and move.

The only thing holding you back from Royal Crown Diamond is you.

It's time to run.

Are you ready?

To the leaders...

You've read Gameplan and are ready to take your team to the next level by investing in your leaders. This workbook is the tool you need to effectively and consistently build into your team. You need to turn the dreams in your head into a moving, growing team. Gameplan is a compilation of many Oil Ability leaders' tried and true methods, all in one place. I found that there was great material out there, but you needed a stack of books to train your team. The Gameplan book and workbook compiles it in an easy to understand format and tailors it directly to your team. It's customized strategy.

Vicki Opfer is a Young Living Royal Crown Diamond that wrote a fantastic document called "Heart Centered Sharing." In it, she lays out numbers of what sharing looks like for her business. She says if you enroll 2 people a month, at the end of the year, you will have a team of 25 and your check will be about 100 dollars higher. But if you enroll 2 people a month and train them how to enroll their own 2 people, (and they in turn train those 2 people how to enroll just 2 people), at the end of the year you have 531,440 people in your organization and a Young Living check of over 10-thousand dollars a month.

It's all in the training.

My hope is that you will take this workbook and use it to train your own teams. We offer bulk pricing on the Gameplan book and workbook at oilabilityteam.com to make your training easy and affordable. If you were to take the Gameplan book and workbook and train just 2 of your top leaders, and then train them how to use it to train their leaders, your organization would grow exponentially.

What does training look like? There are 24 chapters in Gameplan and 24 chapters in the workbook. They were written side by side. Ask your leaders to read a chapter in Gameplan, do the workbook pages for that chapter, then meet and review them. Offer incentives for completing the chapters. Perhaps you do a 24-day bootcamp with your leaders online with both books. Or maybe you opt to take it slower and meet in person or online once a week over 24 weeks. The neat thing is there truly isn't a wrong way of training. Just tailor it to your team with a pace you can handle. By the end of this workbook, you'll have surefire methods of how to market and host classes, develop warm leads, do follow up, train your leaders, and more.

The ultimate goal is to get your leaders to see where this goes. If they write out their dreams and wishes and see that how they are spending their time at their 40-hour-a-week job is not going to get them there, it will not be hard to motivate them to commit 2 hours a week to hold a class. The 2 hours a week, over time, can build into a sustainable business through consistency and tenacity that will replace the 40 hours they are pursuing daily. Your task is to train them how to dream, and where to start.

Then train them how to train their own leaders.

That is the whole key to Gameplan. If you want to see the greatest results, don't keep these books tucked away on a shelf for your eyes only. Use them how they were meant to be used, to inspire and equip your leaders.

Then teach them to how to duplicate.

You have this, Diamond. Get out there and show them how it's done!

My name is

———————————————————————————

And I am a Young Living Royal Crown Diamond.

CHAPTER 1

WHY LAUNCH A YOUNG LIVING BUSINESS

Recap 10 reasons why it's smart to launch a Young Living business. (Hint: Scour the "Why Launch a Young Living Business" chapter in the Gameplan book to find your answers! There are more than 10 reasons!)

1) _____

2) _____

3) _____

4) _____

5) _____

6) _____

7) _____

8) _____

9) _____

10) _____

Which one is your favorite? Circle it.

Check out the Young Living income disclosure guide. Write down a few goals. Write down what that average income would do for your family, and what changes you could make.

I want to make _____ rank by _____ , 20___.

I will have an average income of $_____ a month.

When I attain that rank, I can:

_____

_____

_____

_____

Now vision cast with me. Did you check out the income disclosure guide? That's a tally of what all Young Living distributors everywhere are making. What would you do with a Royal Crown Diamond monthly income of $241,324 dollars?

Write down 3 things that would be on your ultimate bucket list.

1) _____

2) _____

3) _____

Do you believe that's attainable? Tell me the truth! Do you believe network marketing truly works? Do you believe that if you put the hard work in, and be tenacious, and be consistent—that you can get there?

YOUR ASSIGNMENT: WRITE YOUR WHY

Take a few moments and write out your "why". Why are you a Young Living distributor? Be real. When I first started, it truly was just to get the oils in my home. I could not afford them with 5 kids, one special needs son in a pricey school, 70-thousand dollars in student loans, and a mortgage. It then morphed into seeing the miracles around me every day from those oils working. And after about 6 months, my Young Living income surpassed my full time job. That's when I realized I truly had a passion for helping people do what John and I had just done. One year and one month after getting my starter kit, I retired from 18 years of waking up at 3 a.m. for my shift. Two years and two months after getting my starter kit, my husband also came home for good. I was 37 and he was 41. It is possible!

My why now is to raise as many Diamonds as possible. I believe you can truly do what you were called and created to do when you have the time economy and the financial freedom to pour into those around you, and aren't always depleted, operating in emergency mode. That's my why. After living in decades of extreme poverty, my why is to raise as many people out of it as possible. That's why this book isn't just for our team. It's for anyone who has a hope of getting out of their cycle of survival.

It's time for you to put your pencil to the paper. Tell me your why; your hopes and your dreams. Some of mine are:

-to get a little boat and take my kids out on the Fingerlakes of New York where we live. My grandparents had a sailboat when I was growing up, and I went on to get scuba certified at 14 years old and fall in love with the water. I have always wanted my kids to experience some of my memories.

-to take a vacation once a year with all 5 of our kids, and to go away on a weekend every other month alone with my husband that is at least 2 nights long

-to travel and take my homeschoolers with me to explore and see the world

-to pay off every penny of debt we've accrued, our home too, so we can live on 10 percent and tithe 90 percent of our income to ministries that tug on our hearts

-to mentor young couples and single moms so they can have financial freedom

-to visit our family all over the country—and stay longer than a few days

-to rest. To take a week at a time and just read in my hammock and weed my garden and go on long walks in the woods and sleep late and take a nap.

That's my bucket list.

Now tell me your yours. Tell me why you're doing this business. Tell me your dreams. What do you want out of this journey? Be brave. And be real. And truly think it through. Then as you do each of these things, cross them off and write the date that it happened right beside it.

BONUS ASSIGNMENT

If you are still in doubt about network marketing being a wise choice for you, I have an extra assignment for you. I want you to go to one of my favorite network marketer's sites, ericworre.com, and check out his store. His "Go Pro" book is one of my favorite network marketing books of all time, and worth a top-down read. But I have a different assignment for you: I want you to invest in the "Rise of the Entrepreneur" DVD. If you still truly believe your 9 to 5 job is the best way to care for your family, that will be the best 52 minutes you spend this year. It's loaded with statistics and facts about network marketing that will forever change the way you look at the 40-hour work week.

CHAPTER 2

SARAH'S STORY

If you read Gameplan Chapter Two, you have now read my dirt. Every family has dirt. Our family's dirt was alcoholism, drug addiction, mental health, and poverty. I believe that the cycle can be broken. I believe you can change the course of your family's path, by first believing it's possible, then coming up with a plan on how to get from point A to point B, and taking small steps to get there.

YOUR ASSIGNMENT: WRITE YOUR STORY

Take some time and write out your story. Write down where you have been. In bullet points, share some of the hardest moments of your life. Then at the end, I want you to write in the largest letters possible: FAMINE OVER. I AM FREE.

CHAPTER 3

HOW TO BEGIN: A QUICK-START TRAINING GUIDE WITH JUST 2 TIPS

Can it really be that simple? Grab a simple 101 Script, get a few people in front of you and read it? Then rinse and repeat?

I tell you from the deepest places of my heart, there is no magic pill to the rank John and I hit. It was just raw work. It was rolling up my sleeves and getting out there and doing it. You don't need to hit the pavement as hard as I did, but if you commit to 4-6 classes a month (that's about an 8 hour a month time commitment), that's what it's taken for the Silvers on the Oil Ability team to go Silver in Six. We have 11 Silvers on the team at the moment with another 8 set to hit it in the next 4-8 weeks, and every single one of them did it in 6 months, simply by holding 4 classes a month and doing good follow up. Then when someone sold a kit, they immediately trained them using the Teacher Training script in the back of Gameplan.

Is it worth it? Is an extra $2,000 to $3,000 a month worth doing this business alongside your life for a season, until you can drop a few things off your plate? The strategy has been the same from each of the Diamonds I have interviewed. Every time I ask them what the key to their success was, I get the same answer: classes. Class after class after class. There is no chincy way of ranking. You just have to get out there and do it.

YOUR ASSIGNMENT: PREPARE FOR YOUR FIRST CLASS

Photocopy the 101 Script out of the back of the Gameplan book and begin practicing it. It takes about 20 minutes to read it aloud if it's just you and a mirror. If you're doing it in front of someone, it takes about 30 minutes. Read it through 10 times, over 1-2 weeks. On time 10, that's it. You're out of practice. Then it's time to do it in front of someone. (Or several someones).

Place a check mark in a box each time you read through the script to yourself.

Now I want you to pick your mom or best friend, someone who won't laugh if you lose your place, and have at it.

When you make it through your first live audience, get out there and schedule a class. Read it in your living room. Read it at a restaurant with three people over a piece of cheesecake. Once you get over the fear of that first class, and your unknowns are no longer unknown, it's time to take this seriously.

Go to the store and buy a planner. You can buy one at the Dollar Store if you're on a tight budget, or you can order the ibloom planner that I use and love so much (ibloom.co). Commit to going all in. Locate four free locations you can use in the next month. (They can be your living room if you like. That's where my first classes were!) Book them. Set up Facebook events for them. Have 3 different friends invite 50 friends to each of those events. And get out there and start putting some movement to your dreams.

Got all that? Here's review of your homework for this chapter so far:

- ☐ Practice the 101 lecture 10 times
- ☐ Practice it in front of someone you know well who can give you pointers

Now you're ready to actually start! Get your first 4 classes up on Facebook, market them, and have people start inviting. It's go time. If you need wording on how to market your class, take a peek in the Gameplan book.

BONUS ASSIGNMENT: CREATE A VISION BOARD

Prepping for your first class is not the only assignment for this chapter. I also want you to have some tangible dreams you can see every single day, so it keeps you going. Here is your mission: go to a craft store, spend $3 on a canvas board, and spend an afternoon cutting up some magazines. Cut out pictures of your dreams (for me it would be that boat!) Cut out words that you want spoken over your business. Print the rank you want to be off the Young Living website. Pull a check out of your checkbook, write the number you want to see on it for your monthly pay, and sign it with Mary Young's name—and glue that thing with tons of glue on that vision board. Put it where you constantly see it. As you pass it, read the words on the board aloud. Speak life over your dreams. Then, when you are chicken about booking a class, look back at the board and remember why you're doing this. It's because Young Living is a way out. But you have to put the work in and start digging.

Here's a photo of my vision board. I know it sounds chincy to sit there with paper and scissors—you're a grown adult, right? But I'll tell you, there is something magical that happens when you put your dreams to paper. They start to come true. Maybe part of it is that you can see where you are going and you have an end game. Part of it is that you are speaking like this every single day, and there is power in the spoken word. (God created the world with the spoken word—it worked for Him!) You're seeing your goals every single day—and there is power in visualizing where you are heading. Either way, it works. Only six months after making this thing, more than half of it has already happened. Put tangible items on the board, things you know you can do in a year or less. Then move toward the goal.

CHAPTER 4

Avoiding Pitfalls: The 6 Mistakes Every Stagnant Business Builder Makes

List the 6 mistakes I detail in Chapter 4:

1) _____

2) _____

3) _____

4) _____

5) _____

6) _____

Which one do you think is your biggest pitfall?

1) _____

Why? _____

YOUR ASSIGNMENT: FOCUS ON THE SOLUTION

Write up a plan (or several!) for avoiding or overcoming you biggest pitfall. What is the solution to avoiding that mistake? Show me what it looks like for you to learn from my mistakes and avoid these pitfalls. Use phrases like "I will..." and "I won't..."

CHAPTER 5

OVERCOMING EXCUSES AND FINDING YOUR NICHE

I was sneaky in this chapter. I titled it "finding your niche". But truly, it's a chapter that blasts you from the start about defying excuses. Why is identifying them so important? Because it can emotionally cripple your business if you believe lies. I wrote down some of the top excuses I hear in Young Living. In fact, I listed 11 different excuses in the opening to the chapter. Can you identify some of them again, with the response to each excuse?

I am sure you've heard all those excuses before. But tell me which one you think describes you the most:

YOUR ASSIGNMENT: MOVE BEYOND YOUR EXCUSES

Now I want you to write down you way out of it. What is the opposite of that statement above? How can you fight your own negativity in your head? Walk me through it by writing it down. If you cannot think of a way out of that thought pattern, simply write down the opposite.

Example: "I don't know anyone." Opposite: "I do have a friend circle of _____ people, and it is growing every day. I will be successful at this, because I am a Young Living Diamond. A Diamond does not make excuses. They cut through mountains. I am finding a way around my mountain without a word of complaint, because I know where my hard work will lead me. And it's worth the fight."

_____

_____

_____

_____

_____

Now to the second part of the chapter. There are many ways of sharing Young Living. While I still believe with all my heart that in-person classes with as many people as you can is the fastest way to grow, I know that's not possible for everyone in every season. Check by the options below that you believe you may be good at.

- ☐ mailing out DVD's or audio CD's from oilabilityteam.com and doing good follow up

- ☐ having an eye for talent and raising business builders

- ☐ putting oils on people. Handing out samples and doing good follow up

- ☐ meeting people one on one over your lunch break or for dinner and going over the 101 lecture

- ☐ putting up flyers at local businesses and connecting with the owners to hold classes at chiropractic offices, natural food stores, bulk food stores, Yoga studios, and more

- ☐ writing, blogging, and vlogging online. Doing online Facebook live or zoom or blab classes. Marketing heavily before and doing great follow up after

- ☐ hand written notes, flyers and samples. You're a gifted letter writer

☐ an eye for sales. Learning to work paid leads and prospects and branching out to new people you've never met

☐ tithing and praying and letting the Lord grow your business organically, but acting deliberately on every single person He puts in your path

You may have circled one or two. I'll tell you straight up I've used every single one of these methods. And they all work. In-person classes work the fastest. But if you need a place to start, and you see another gifting in yourself, go for it. Use one of the other methods above. The key is being consistent, working your business as a business, and doing knockout follow up.

If people sense that you are real and they are not being hunted solely for a starter kit, and you can pass along your passion, you will grow.

My advice is to diversify. In the span of a month, do three in-person classes, give it a shot at an online class, and get oils on people. Get into a vendor event and meet some new faces. Use all the methods. But make sure they all have a component of the 101 Script in them, or you won't get results.

Let me flesh that out for you for a bit. If you do a specialty class like a beauty school, incorporate some of the 101 notes while they are doing their facials and have the masque on, and make sure you tell them where to get the starter kit. If you are doing a make-and-take class, make them watch a 10-minute version of the 101 class on a DVD before you start—maybe something you shoot ahead of time. If you are doing a vendor event, hand out 101 audio CD's to every person that fills out a form to win a gift basket. (They cost about a dollar each). If you give someone an oil at work to help them out, practice the "if I, would you" mentality (see Chapter 12 of Gameplan for this strategy) and ask them if you give them the oil for free, wwould they listen to the audio 101 CD on the way home from work in the car? Always make sure there's a response from the person you are working with—or your work is for naught.

Can I throw in one more thing? It's a principle that I think is very important, because I get requests weekly for people wanting to jump ship with the team they are on and move to the Oil Ability team. It drives me crazy. If you are not successful where you are, you won't be successful on our team. How do I know? Success depends on you. It has nothing to do with your upline, how much you know, how kind the people are around you, how much support you have, or how many resources you are given. Blaming your upline is another excuse.

There is a wonderful quote in Eric Worre's "Go Pro" book that I love. (It's a fantastic book that will help you with the emotional side of network marketing—pick it up at ericworre.com and give it a good read.) I'd like you not just to read this paragraph, but to write it on a 3x5 card and put it on your bathroom mirror, and repeat it to yourself when you see it. You have no one to blame for your failure but you.

From page 103 of his book:

"If I succeed in this business, it's going to be me that creates the success, not my upline. And if I fail in this business, it's going to be me that creates the failure, not my team or my upline. I am the difference between success and failure. My upline is here to guide me, but they cannot do the work for me. They are here to work with me, but not for me."

CHAPTER 6

YOUR GREATEST TOOL: A DETAILED TOUR OF THE YOUNG LIVING VIRTUAL OFFICE

For this one, you'll have to go tech savy on me. Before you go any further in this book, find your username and password (the one you wrote down when you bought your starter kit.) If you can't find it, call Young Living directly and they'll issue you a new password—it's super easy.

Once you have that, go to youngliving.com and click "sign in." Then you'll be at the screen where you'll need that username and password. Every single person that gets a starter kit, whether they are selling or not, should have been trained by their upline to log in and check out their virtual office. At the very least, they have to know how to order more product. My advice is to scope out 2 buttons first. At the top in the center is the "Getting Started" tab. It's loaded with 3 and 4-minute videos that will really lay the groundwork for your understanding of Young Living. It's important that you spend some time on Young Living's Seed to Seal site (one of the links on the Getting Started page). It is what sets us apart from every other oils company in the world.

If you want to kick it up a notch, and really want to understand why Young Living is a pioneer, go to "Quick Order" and type in "D. Gary Young: The World Leader In Essential Oils". A book with a purple cover will pop up with a photo of Gary on it. If you read that book, it will put to rest any question in your mind about the stewardship and integrity of Young Living, and what it took to become a billion dollar oils company. My eyes still well up when I look at what Gary went through to bring us the purest oils in the world. It was such an incredible journey. For those of you that think Gameplan has sucked all the brain cells out of your brain, don't dismay. This book is mostly pictures. It's a picture journey of Young Living's story.

Back to the Virtual Office. After you've watched all the videos in the "Getting Started" tab, it's time to do some reading online. The next tab I want you to check out is "Member Resources." That one is loaded with documents to read. Hone in on "Policies and Procedures" and devour it. Those are all the rules of Young Living. For example, did you know that you can't sign your spouse and get two Young Living checks in your home, unless they were already a distributor before you were married? It's good to know those rules. Print them off, put them in a binder, read them once, and move on.

When you have a lazy afternoon, just click through all the other tabs under Member Resources. Get familiar with the powerpoint presentations, Young Living University, and all the shareable graphics and FDA compliance information. There is SO much on that tab.

Once you're done with those 2 buttons, grab Gameplan and follow along. Click on the buttons across the top of your dashboard and the buttons to the left, following the graphics in the book, and become familiar with where everything is.

Got all that? Let me lay it out again:

YOUR ASSIGNMENT: GET FAMILIAR WITH THE VIRTUAL OFFICE

☐ Click on the "Getting Started" tab and watch all the videos

☐ Order the "D. Gary Young: The World Leader In Essential Oils" book off the Quick Order button and read it (it's worth it!)

☐ Click on "Member Resources" and lose yourself in all the resources they have pooled together for us

☐ Open your Gameplan book and go to Chapter 6 and the Virtual Office tour, and click through each of the buttons across the top and left side of the virtual office, getting familiar with where things are.

Make sure you understand the Rank Qualification button. I'm on that myself a couple of times a day. It's your end game. It's your goal post. It's where you're heading. You're never going to get where you're going if you don't know what the end game is. Set a goal, perhaps a small one at first, and chart it under that button.

For those of you that picked up this workbook, I am going to give you a little bonus section not in the Gameplan book as a thank you. Because you are going through the "Rank Qualification button", I want to talk you through early in the workbook on exactly how to rank up.

BONUS TRAINING: RANKING STRATEGIES

In this section I'm going to go a little deeper into the ranking strategies I laid out in Gameplan. If you are a details person and really want more examples of what it looks like to apply a winning strategy to building your business, this bonus training is just for you.

I know it's easy to see Star rank and set your sites on that, with little beyond. But those first two ranks (Star and Senior Star) are just there to get your attention. They're there to show you that you can do this—to give you vision. The first true goal you need to have in mind is to hit Executive, even from the very beginning. There is a reason for this. The whole foundation of the start of your business stems from that. From the moment you make a decision to be a Young Living distributor, put your sights on Executive so you have your chess pieces in the right places to rank even higher. According to the "rank qualification" tab, you need a PGV of 1000, an overall OGV of 4000, and 2 legs with 1000 OGV in each.

Before I give you more strategy, do the homework assignment below so you know what I'm talking about.

Tell me what a few terms mean so you can learn Young Living-ease. (If you need a hint, there is a Young Living-ease glossary in Appendix M of Gameplan to help you out.)

OGV: _____

PGV: _____

Upline: _____

Downline: _____

Legs: _____

Essential Rewards: _____

Why do you want to be on ER? (This is one of the key secrets to ranking up!)

_____

_____

What it takes to attain the rank of silver: (OGV, PGV, legs):

_____

_____

Back to strategy.

From the first moment of your business, I want you to be looking for two leaders. For the first month or two, depending on how many classes you hold each month, just sign everyone under you. You are the sponsor and you are the enroller. You are waiting to see who "pops"—who turns around and sells a kit to someone else. That may be your first leader. Get them trained—stat—while they are on fire—with the Teacher Training in the Appendix of the Gameplan book. Then gift the Gameplan book to them after their first class as a reward, so they can start their oily business on the right foot.

If no one "pops" after your first 8 classes or so, I want you to continue signing people under you directly until 1 of 2 things happens: you reach 1000PGV (that's volume outside your 2 legs), or you pick up another business builder that's willing to let you host classes for them and is spending the 100pv a month to get a paycheck.

Why do you need loose people (non-business builders) under you? What exactly is PGV? It's your Personal Group Volume—the sales that come from people on your team who aren't in a qualifying leg. It's five or six people under you on Essential Rewards, ordering each month. They have no one under them. They are just loose members on your team.

Once you have 1000 PGV established, every single kit sale from that point on goes under one of two people who are going to be your legs. Your first goal is Executive: that's 4000 OGV volume, and 10 kits on each of those two legs. Ideally, those two leaders are working in tandem with you and you're leaning on their friend circles to pull off classes.

The benefit to building this way is:

1) Your PGV will be established and you'll never have to worry about it again, all the way to Royal Crown Diamond. You must have 1000 PGV at all times or you lose your check once you hit Silver. You will have laid the groundwork.

2) You'll have two leaders to build under, the same two that you need to hit the next rank of Silver.

How do you know who to place where? I just go back and forth between the two legs, and keep them at about the same volume. If one of your legs is at 400 OGV and the other is at 800 OGV, I'd be teaching under the 400 OGV rank because you need it at 1000 OGV to rank.

So here are the steps again, in layman's terms:

For your first 2 months or 8 classes, sign everyone under you as both sponsor and enroller. The goal is to build up 1000 PGV, $1000 in sales outside your two legs.

During this time, watch to see who "pops". If someone pops right away, and you're teaching four classes a month, teach one or two classes for them, and the other two classes would go for your PGV—so they would go directly under you.

If you teach for two months and have no leaders, have a good conversation with the people you have gotten on Essential Rewards that are excited about the oils. If they don't want a business, ask if they are willing to allow you to teach and build legs under them—so they can get their oils for free. If their answer is yes, then start using them as sponsor and you as enroller. Their requirement would be to spend 100 PV a month to get paid, and to open their friend circle to you. The payoff is free oils!

Once your PGV is established, all your attention goes on those two leaders. Every person goes under one of those two legs, and nowhere else, to help you get to Executive. From day one, your eye is on that rank, so you have your foundation laid for Silver and your PGV is in place.

One more tip: from the beginning, plug the business! I have never had a hard time finding business builders, because from my first class I was telling people why Young Living was the best job I'd ever had. Even if you just drop two or three lines in your 101 class, it will spark interest. Another way to raise business builders is to chase every 101 class with the 10 minute "Why Do Young Living as a Business" DVD on our website, oilabilityteam.com. It's amazing who moves on what they see—it's rarely the person I pick out of the crowd!

You have survived your only techie tour in this workbook! Congratulations! The rest of the book is much less strenuous on your brain!

CHAPTER 7

YOUNG LIVING MARKETING 101: HOW TO SHARE THE OILS

What is the truth about network marketing? Share it with me below.

_____

_____

_____

Now, I want you to go to Youtube and watch a Pat Petrini video called "I Still Think It's A Pyramid Scheme." It's 3 minutes of your life that you'll never get back. But you'll love me for it. No one will ever be able to tell you that network marketing is a pyramid scheme again. You can find it by typing "I think it's a pyramid scheme" into the search engine on Youtube. After a few giggles, tell me what you learned.

_____

_____

_____

I'm going to have you do a few outline exercises, because it's good for your soul. Finish these thoughts right out of the Gameplan book:

Never once have I _____

There are two things you need _____

You don't need to become _____

The trick isn't _____

_____

Great job! Now that you know Network Marketing is the real deal, I want you to walk me through the 8 steps to set up a Facebook event. It's time to get your first class on the road. You can't get off the ground if you don't teach.

1) _____

_____

2) _____

_____

3) _____

_____

4) _____

_____

5) _____

_____

6) _____

_____

7) _____

_____

8) _____

_____

YOUR ASSIGNMENT: PRACTICE MARKETING AN EVENT

Now go to Facebook and try setting up your own event. Don't spend a lot of time getting the wording just right—we're gonna work on that in the next chapter. For now just practice uploading a banner and getting a few lines in the description box. Don't worry, no one will see your practice event unless you take the final step of inviting people! This is just so that you learn how to do this, and see how easy it is! When you have a description handy and a photo selected for the banner, it only takes about two minutes to set up an event.

Now tell me, what are the 4 steps to simple marketing?

1) _____

2) _____

3) _____

4) _____

What are the 9 steps to holding an online class?

1) _____

2) _____

3) _____

4) _____

5) _____

6) _____

7) _____

8) _____

9) _____

BONUS ASSIGNMENT: FILM AN ONLINE CLASS INTRO

For the bold leaders out there: grab your cell phone, grab the first paragraph of the 101 Script, find a well-lit place without an echo, and try recording it. Just do a dry run. See what you look like on camera. Critique yourself. You can do this! Make sure the video is no longer then 3-4 minutes.

You now you see that you have everything it takes to shoot an entire 101 and upload it online. You can do this!

What about vendor events?

Go into them with the expectation of getting leads for classes, not selling oodles of starter kits. Write down 2 tips that you picked up from this section:

1) _____

_____

2) _____

_____

Talking to Cold Contacts

What did you think about the role playing exercise to gain business builders? I have had so many conversations just like that! The last 3 business builders I signed this week I met in random places: in airports, in restaurants, at the post office. It just takes a heart to see that people are dissatisfied.

- ☐ Try reading it through again imagining you're pitching it to someone you truly love, that you want to see set free from financial bondage.

- ☐ Practice the role play a few times so it's in your head when you come across someone who will be playing the other end live.

YOUR ASSIGNMENT: MAKE A LIST

This next assignment is going to take you a while. In fact, for people who like to walk away from a workbook and have it completely finished, this assignment is really going to irk you- because it's never quite done.

Today, I want you to start compiling a list of your warm market. In network marketing terms, these are people that know you—perhaps very well, like a family member, or just as an acquaintance. If they hear your name and they know who you are, they are your warm market.

For the first week, I want you to be really deliberate about putting this list together. After that, I want you to keep your workbook in a place where you have access to it regularly, and every time you come across someone you forgot, add their name to the list. After a month or so, leave your workbook at home and just text names to yourself of people that need to be on this list.

I set aside 5 pages of lines for you to write names, though you may end up needing far more. These are the people that you'll use to invite 50 people to your class events set up on Facebook, or when you have plateaued, to do one-on-one classes with.

Let me give you some ideas of where to draw from. Take the next few pages and make a list of every single person you know that should be introduced to oils. (That was a trick question. EVERY person you know should be introduced to oils.)

Start with Facebook. Go through your entire friend's list and add most of the names. Then go through your other social media outlets: Instagram, Pinterest, Twitter, your email account, LinkedIn, Snapchat, and any other place you may be connecting with people online.

After that, I usually comb through my address book—the one I use when I mail Christmas cards. Look through you cell phone for contacts you may have forgotten and add them. Think through the people you see at church, in small group, in your homeschool group or any activity for your kids at public school, in boy scouts, ballet, soccer, basketball, football, band, art club, or cheerleading.

Think about the paths you cross at the post office, and the woman that has sent your packages 40 times that knows your face. Think about your co-workers. Think about the neighbors on your street. Then think of your friends, and the friends they have had to their homes while you have been there. Think of all the people you run into doing the things that you love: running, reading, volunteering—any place your feet may go. Think of all your ties in the community: the chamber of commerce, the 5k that you ran, the car wash you took part in. Think about all your acquaintances that you see in passing, your spouse's coworkers and the friend that is always at your friend's home when you go over there.

Literally make a working list of every human you know. And put them on these next few sheets. When you are frustrated and can't fill classes, this is the place I want you to return to for inspiration. There are always people that have been missed for starter kits. One of the worst feelings in the world is seeing an old friend sign with someone they don't even know—because you never made contact with them. This is how to stop that from happening.

Why you need a list

Let me tell you a story. After I ranked Platinum, I got stuck there for 5 months. My OGV hovered between 120,000 and 150,000 every month. So I decided to take my own advice and take another look at my warm market (the people that I knew personally). What I discovered was that in my rush to diamond, I had totally left out some of my closest friends. Because I have a business Facebook page and do most of my oils posts there, there were people in my own family- close cousins, aunts, best friends—that had never been introduced to oils.

When you have a product that you deeply believe in, don't you want your family and friends to have it first? In my haste, I had forgotten the people I most loved. I had taught 182 classes in New York and Pennsylvania and completely left out the town I grew up in, the place I lived for 30 years: Chicago. So one morning, I sat down and made a list of my Chicago contacts only. 450 people. If I sold a kit to those people alone, I would have half the volume to get to diamond without another leader selling single kit. And my closest friends would be on my oils team.

Do not forget those closest to you. The worst thing that can happen is that they sign on another oils team because you never spoke up. It would hurt to have your best friend somewhere else! So be bold. Speak out. Have no fear.

And make your list. Right now. When you are done, contact 5 of those people every week. Start with a relationship. Listen to where they are. Form them to get to know their needs. And meet them where they are on their road.

Once you have thought of every person you know, carry this book with you for a while and keep adding names as you think of new places and faces. Then pick it up every few weeks and add to it. The list will be much longer then you thought it would.

One. Two. Three... GO.

You don't need to be an expert

There is just one more thing I want to throw in at the end of Chapter 7, because it's a roadblock to so many distributors. We hit it right at the end of the chapter. You don't need to be an expert to do network marketing.

For most of my life, people have relied on me as a news anchor to provide them with trustworthy, accurate information. In fact—they even rely on me to provide information that I have no idea about, like the weather forecast (never once have I been to a school for meteorology!) But here's the secret to being a news anchor: you just have to get really good at finding stuff. When I come into a newsroom, I first read about 39 newspapers online (I am speed reading folks, I am not THAT good), and I read 6 papers that are delivered to the door. Then I watch the networks—all 7 of them. By the time I go on, I know where the best soundbites are, the best facts, and the strongest writing. I have seen it all by 6 a.m. and I can see my entire shift in my head. I know what angle I will take my newscasts from.

That's sort of the way a Young Living business works. You don't need to download 100 years of aromatherapy and be an M.D. to make it work. Actually, even if you went for those credentials, you'd still not be able to share in the way that you want to, because once you are a distributor, you are an extension of Young Living Corporate, and you fall under all of the rules and regulations that the staff fall under because of the FDA. You are not allowed to use the oils to treat diseases. Titles mean nothing. Believe me though, it's a much better title to have distributor after your name, and know where that goes, then to go for a certification that won't bring the pay, relationships, time freedom, and growth you'll get from teaching classes and building a team. A distributorship is always the right way to go.

If your heart is to help people, the best thing you can do is get really good at understanding third party resources. Take a moment and list some of the top resources I've laid out for you below:

☐ _____

☐ _____

☐ _____

If there is one thing I want you to get out of this chapter, it's that you truly don't need to be an expert. You just need passion to share the oils. Compassion for where people are, without judgment. And tenacity to see it through to the end. Learn your tools and leave the expert advice to the experts. Then you'll rock Young Living.

CHAPTER 8

THE OIL ABILITY MARKETING SYSTEM: HOW TO FILL CLASSES WITHOUT KNOWING PEOPLE

Let's play a fill-in-the-blank game for this chapter, because so many of the concepts are terribly important for you to cut down on discouragement.

The trick to filling classes isn't who you know, it's _____

_____

The average person knows about _____

It's going to take a lot more than just you _____

_____

What is the Oil Ability Event Marketing System? Write it out.

1) _____

2) _____

3) _____

4) _____

5) _____

6) _____

Not convinced that you should be on Facebook? For 10 minutes, go to Youtube and type in "21st Century Social Media Trends." The information in that powerful video will astound you. And you'll want to get into social media. If your religious or moral beliefs prohibit it, don't sweat it. Young Living was successful as a company long before Facebook was ever created. Just keep doing in-person classes and great follow up, and you will get where you want to go.

Now let's work on writing. If you're a pretty rotten writer, don't sweat it. Gameplan has just saved you. Go ahead and steal my scripts and marketing. (You're not actually stealing it—you paid for it, silly. If you resell it, I will hunt you down, though.)

YOUR ASSIGNMENT: MARKET YOUR FIRST CLASS

If you think you do a pretty good job at getting your thoughts on paper, then you'll enjoy this homework assignment.

Take some time to write a (short) knockout paragraph to convince people to come to your 101 class. The good news is that you really only need to write it once, because you're always inviting 3 different people to invite 50 people to your classes. Your invitees should always be different, so there's no need to re-invent the wheel, unless you're teaching a different class outside the 101. (And I don't recommend that if you're just starting your business. Once you get people on Essential Rewards, I'll teach one specialty class to keep them interested and give them ideas. But my other 3 classes a month are always prospecting—always looking for new people on my team. The ratio is 3 101's to 1 specialty class, like Oils of the Bible or .)

Back to writing. (You thought you got out of it, didn't you??)

Give me a paragraph that will get someone who has never heard of essential oils into a seat in your class. Be enthusiastic and confident!

Now your task is to actually put this entire chapter into play. Get online, use that paragraph you wrote, set up an event and get 3 people to invite 50 people to it. Go on. Try it.

It's important that you don't just create an event and ask people to share it to their page. There is good marketing and there is bad marketing. Sharing an event is bad marketing—because people won't see any of your posts in the event unless they have actually been invited. It's the same thing if you're running a business page. I see people all the time put a ton of work into posting all day long, and they have 17 people on their page. Dude—if you only have 18 people on your business page, you should be plugging that page constantly (sharing a link to your business page) on your personal page, to garner interest.

☐ Put a check on that box once you've set up your first event. If you have the writing already done (which you do, because you did it above), you can get this sucker up in 10 minutes flat.

Do you need an image for the banner? Hop on over to Oil Ability with Sarah on Facebook, like my page (did you pick up on my marketing there? That was a savvy slip!) Then you have access to all my photos. Click on "photos" and take whatever you like—banner images, etc.... All of it is compliant.

Once that event is up, post in it once or twice a day using the photos from my Facebook page, or any other compliant source you have, like the Young Living blog (which is FANTASTIC.)

You should have 4-6 of these event set up every single month. I market them at the same time every day, first thing in the morning. You can even schedule your posts, so you don't have to be online at 12 noon to pop something up.

What If I Still Can't Fill Classes?

- ☐ listen to your warm market
- ☐ host classes in a public place
- ☐ be willing to travel
- ☐ teach online classes
- ☐ get more personal with your follow up and your invitations to class—have face-to-face interaction
- ☐ incorporate vendor events

Have you tried all the methods of filling classes? If you are stuck, try one of the methods above and see if it gets you moving again. From time to time, I tweak what I'm doing depending on what's going on in my life at the time, and if I feel my business has stalled. Always stay open to all options.

What did you think about the conversations in Chapter 8? The ones that give you an idea of how to invite someone—in 30 seconds flat—to your class? Or to catch a business builder's attention?

Return to those conversations and read them again in the Gameplan book, especially if you struggle with face-to-face interaction, or feel like you are forcing someone to make a decision.

☐ Go read them through three times today.

Familiarize yourself with a running script in your head, so it automatically rolls off your tongue when you need it but can't think of what to say.

CHAPTER 9

ANATOMY OF A SUCCESSFUL CLASS

What are the top 3 take-aways you got from the tips on how to have a successful class?

1) _____

2) _____

3) _____

Nailing the close

The close is the hardest thing to master. It's the part of the lecture where you generally feel like you're coming off salesy. But I truly want you to imagine something completely different. Your close comes down to your mindset, and nothing else. If you go into it with the goal of selling starter kits, you'll always come off salesy. If you go into it with a genuine goal of educating people and helping them to make better choices, you'll never lose.

Listen to the difference:

Starter kit mentality:

You HAVE to get the starter kit tonight. It's the best deal on Young Living's site. It's the only thing on their site that's half off. It comes with 11 bottles of oil and a diffuser. You can't get it that cheap in the store!

I do typically have a paragraph like the one above in my close. I but usually begin with something like this:

Education Mindset:

There are over 185,000 known chemicals actively used in products in the United States today. The average person puts 300 chemicals a day on their skin through 4 things: soap, shampoo, makeup and haircare. 80 of those chemicals are used before breakfast. The FDA says to date, less than 15 percent of all chemicals in the U.S. have been thoroughly studied for their side effects. Common side effects of chemical uses: endocrine disruptors, which make you gain weight, skin issues, asthma, and even cancer. There is a better way to get the poison out of your home. It comes down to making smarter decisions. What's in an oil? Lemon. Peppermint. Tangerine. Sage. No yuck. No chemicals. Nothing that will poison your body. I'd like to issue a 3-cabinet challenge: go home, pick 3 cabinets in your house, and read the ingredients that are in the products you're using. Look in your laundry room. Look under your kitchen sink and in your bathroom. If you can't pronounce it, why are you using it?

You can't control all of the toxins you'll be exposed to. But you can draw a line in the sand and say "no more" when it comes to what is found within the walls of your own home. Make a better choice today. Make the switch to oils. Oils for your deodorant instead of deodorant with aluminum. Oils in your toothpaste instead of toothpaste with fluoride. Switch out your glass cleaner and multi-surface cleaner with Thieves cleaner. Use Thieves laundry soap to get rid of your laundry soap with sodium laurel sulfate in it—known to cause cancer. There is a better way. Start with 1 small step at a time; one small swap each month. A chemical free home is a safer home.

Do you see the difference? One is in for the sale. They are on the hunt. The other is compassionately teaching. Anyone who leaves will be thinking about what's in their house. They won't be thinking you're selling to them. They'll be thinking you care about them by educating them. And if you do good follow up, you'll have another member on your team.

Take a few moments and try writing your own close to the 101 lecture. Incorporate your (FDA compliant) stories. Pull from the close above and the two closes in the back of the Gameplan book to come up with your own way to end your classes.

I'm going to have you do a bit more writing than just that. But don't stress about it—you only have to do it once, because you'll reuse it for every single class. A few sentences are enough—it need not be long.

One leader on my team told me she'd held off using my 101 Script for over two years, because she felt like it wasn't "hers." But when she read through this workbook and realized she could customize it, so it was in her own words with her own stories, suddenly she didn't feel as if she was relying on me to teach her classes for her. She said "just a few tweaks, and I felt like I owned it. It was amazing what my story added to the lecture. I am now confident that

I'm not just reading Sarah's work to them, I am educating them—using my own story. Just a few lines made all the difference for me." (By the way, after 2 years of sitting on her business, in one fall, Kimarie is now an Executive, well on her way to Silver.)

For this chapter, I want you to write one paragraph that tells (compliantly) your Young Living story. Why did you get into oils? Think about that place you were at before you'd ever smelled an essential oil. Think about where you are now and the things you have learned. Show them it's one of the best choices you have made. Tell your story. Tell your why. That's how you will open your class.

For the second page, write your close. You can take one of the closing pages from the Appendix of the Gameplan book, or have your own. The most important component is that the people in the class get to smell the starter kit, and you show them where to order. Write out how you want to say it. It doesn't need to come off salesy—it can be something as simple as "I started my Young Living journey with a Premium Starter kit. That's where I'd recommend you begin, too—because you get 24 percent off your oils for life once you have that kit in your hands. It's the best deal out there. Let me show you how to navigate the website, for anyone wanting to sign up tonight. It takes 10 minutes."

- ☐ 1—write your open. Your story.
- ☐ 2—write your close. Know your end game.

YOUR STORY.

YOUR CLOSE

CHAPTER 10

THE OIL ABILITY FOLLOW UP SYSTEM

What are the three types of people you'll encounter when you do follow up?

1) _____

2) _____

3) _____

What do you do with the people who are not interested? _____

_____

_____

What about with the people who say they can't afford it?_____

_____

_____

What are they really telling you? _____

_____

_____

Explain the Hinterkopf method of getting in touch with people after class.

_____

_____

_____

_____

Consistency will make or break your business. It's absolutely critical that you set aside established times for you to work. When I first started teaching while I was still anchoring news, I taught 4 classes a month, but I knew I needed some weekends off to be able to function as a homeschool mom with a job that started at 3 a.m. So I taught Friday and Saturday, then took the next weekend off. I'd rinse and repeat. Friday and Saturday, with the next weekend off. With that structure, I built to Silver and beyond.

What does a Young Living work week look like for you? Write out the nights you see yourself being able to consistently teach each week, and the hours in the week you could dedicate to following up and doing mailings.

_____

_____

_____

_____

_____

_____

_____

_____

Write down how many hours you're willing to commit to grow your business to a Silver level. Now I want you to track your hours—right here—over the next 4 weeks—to hold yourself accountable. You don't have to do it every single month, but do it for the first month. They say that if you can consistently do something for 30 days, you will have made a habit of it, and it will come more easily to you.

The number of hours you can commit each week: _____

Now I want to you hold yourself accountable on an even deeper level, beyond your hours. For the next 12 weeks, write the dates of your classes on these next few lines. See if you can stick to the goals you're setting. If not, it's time to revise the goals or revisit your "why" to get inspired and get out there.

Classes for week 1:_____

Classes for week 2:_____

Classes for week 3:_____

Classes for week 4: _____

Classes for week 5:_____

Classes for week 6:_____

_____

Classes for week 7:_____

_____

Classes for week 8:_____

_____

Classes for week 9:_____

_____

Classes for week 10: _____

_____

Classes for week 11: _____

_____

Classes for week 12: _____

_____

It's good to write the dates of your classes down, but it's also good to see them visually mapped out by month. This is a good example from one of my Silvers of how she tracks her team's classes on Facebook:

This is our November Calendar. The number one way to build your business is to TEACH! Who's got classes scheduled this month? Please share your calendars!

November 2016 Class Schedule – Team DeValk

You can easily design and print off your own calendars online for free using the website www.wincalendar.com (as listed above). I also like the ibloom.co personal planners, they are wonderful for tracking your business. Your task this week is to get 4 classes on the calendar for next month, and get 3 people to invite to those classes through Facebook events that you have set up.

YOUR ASSIGNMENT: PLAN TO FOLLOW UP

Once you have you classes scheduled, I want you to check out Appendix C in this workbook. It gives you wonderful 3x5 cutout cards that you can tape to index cards and keep in a card file alphabetically to track the people you have personally enrolled. The cards tell you exactly which questions to ask. I print them out and track every person that gets a kit with me as enroller.

☐ Print the cards so you're prepared for the follow up you'll be doing.

CHAPTER 11

DEALING WITH DIFFICULT PEOPLE

Give an example of enabling. _____

_____

_____

What should you do when they only want one oil? _____

_____

_____

How do you handle people who are negative about oils? _____

_____

_____

The trick is to emotionally separate yourself from the naysayers. When your identity is in what you do, you'll always have discouragement because you're basing it on performance. When your identity is in Christ, there is no pressure—because you can do all things through Christ who strengthens you. (Not a few things, all things.) Nothing is impossible. That means you kick the dust off your feet at each no, don't wear it as a discouragement, and move on.

YOUR ASSIGNMENT: CHANGE YOUR ATTITUDE

As you go through your week, try to put this into practice. Write down an example (it may not even be oils related) where you were able to walk away from conflict with a positive attitude.

BONUS ASSIGNMENT: BECOME A CONFIDENT ENTREPRENEUR

Do you need a little more science behind the decision to do network marketing? Do you need a little more convincing? Go to ericworre.com and pick up his "Rise of the Entrepreneur" DVD. It's 50 minutes long, and jam-packed with fact-filled science on this profession. If you're ever worried about where it goes, don't be. The stats don't lie. Just put one foot in front of the other, despite the naysayers, knowing what you are doing will bless your family. As long as you believe this is possible, it is.

CHAPTER 12

No One Is Coming to Classes- Now What?

Because everyone in the world needs oils, each person has an average friend circle of 1000 people, and there are thousands of Silvers and above with the same skill set and resources that you have, I'd say the issue is not who you know or your resources. The issue is how people are perceiving you.

YOUR ASSIGNMENT: CHANGE YOUR PERCEPTION

I want to run you through a quick exercise. I know I already made you read the 101 Script 10 times, but I want you to read it through one more time. At least read the first paragraph.

For the first time through, just do a quick dry read. Read it as though you're giving it at class tonight.

Now I'm going to take you through a visual exercise. I want you to imagine that you are a Young Living Royal Crown Diamond. On the 20th this month, $245,000 will be deposited into your bank account. You are debt free. Your family members and closest friends are cared for. You give generously. You are living comfortably. And you've had that income for 10 years. Next month, another $275,000 will be deposited into your account!

Would you carry yourself differently? Would you have more confidence? Would you treat people with more grace or live on the ragged edge? Would you be well rested? Would you take care of your body? Would you set aside more time for family and friends? Would you live in fear? Would you be afraid of the future?

I want you to live as though you're already there. Envision yourself in that place. Speak with confidence. Hold your head high, because you did the grunt work to earn that rank. Nothing was handed to you. You know what it takes to run a multi-million-dollar network marketing business.

Now go read the first paragraph of your 101 lecture. Read it like you've sold 1000 starter kits. Read it like everyone says yes and everyone respects what you have to say.

THAT is how you should read that lecture.

One other tactic I want to give you is the Eric Worre "If I, will you" principle. It's fantastic, and Worre is a network marketing genius.

Don't ever hand things out to people without expecting something in return. I use this principle all the time with my business builders. You'll notice in the back of Gameplan there is Teacher Training guide on how to raise leaders. I have personally trained over 800 leaders in one year with that system. There are seven homework assignments they must complete (which takes them through one full cycle of a Young Living business: marketing, filling classes, teaching, and follow up). Only then can they earn more materials from me to grow their business. (I personally recommend you give them the Gameplan book and workbook as a reward, but I am biased...) Here's how I use the "If I, will you" tactic with my leaders:

"If I give you 7 homework assignments in exchange for a Gameplan book and workbook, will you complete them?"

It really weeds out the people who say they will do something from the people who actually get out there and do it. You are one of those people who actually gets out there and does it, because you've made it halfway through the workbook and Gameplan, the hardest Young Living strategy book out there.

Here's another example of "If I, will you?"

"If I give you this 101 lecture on audio cd, will you listen to it in your car?"

Now you practice writing an "if I will you" statement, based on something you would hand out.

Great job! The last step to that trick is following up. Set a date where you can check in and make sure they actually did the work. Then if you're looking to sell a starter kit, that's the time to approach them with your close or with getting to a 101 lecture in a live class.

BONUS STRATEGY: HOW TO CONQUER A PLATEAU

There are two other tactics to try if you are having a hard time getting people to class.

Tactic number one: One on one's

Go back to that list of all the people you know, and sit down with them, one or two a week, and start signing people up by meeting with them alone over lunch or dinner. It's amazing how this can help your morale when you plateau. Just keep at it. Never give up.

Those relationships will lead to open doors that explode your business later. You never know who that one person is that ends up being a Diamond beneath you. How do you do a one-on-one? Exactly the same way you do a class with 15 people in it. Grab the 3-page 101 lecture, and read it. Do good follow up. When you touch base, ask if they are willing to host with their friend circle. And watch it grow. My sister had to do one-on-ones for the first 9 months of her business. She had moved to New York from Chicago and had no friend circle because she was working 3 jobs—80 hours a week. She had no personal time to develop relationships, so for months, she used her lunch break for one-on-one's. She eventually signed enough people that she developed a friend circle through their circles. She's now a Silver in Six, and two-thirds of the way to Gold. Keep at it, and never give up. The only thing that kills your business is not doing anything with your business.

Tactic number two: Vendor Events

This is a great way to generate leads. Why isn't a great way to sell kits? Because the average person at a vendor booth will spend less than 60 seconds at your booth as they are perusing. It's really hard to get the enthusiasm going to make a purchase in under 60 seconds. But vendor events are gold if you have no friend circle, because they generate leads. A lead is a person who might come to or host a class.

Here are a few extra pointers in addition to the vendor event tips in Gameplan:

–have your starter kit front and center, right smack dab in the middle of the booth, eye level. Use levels (like $10 crates) to get it right in front of their face. You don't want anyone walking away without the smell of an oil in their nose.

–make sure you have a collection system. It's critical you're collecting their information to generate interest in classes. If you don't have this, you have just wasted your time at the event. I usually do this by offering an oils gift basket as a raffle, and collecting people's names on clipboards to win it. If you want the sign up sheet I place on the clipboard, check out the Appendix on Vendor Events in the Gameplan book.

–it's critical that you have some type of a 30-second script memorized. It's the spiel that you give each person that comes to the booth. You will say it three hundred times a day at a vendor event—the exact same paragraph. It should tell them:

- ☐ what oils are
- ☐ why they want them in their life
- ☐ where they can start

If you need an idea of how to put that together, my vendor script looks something like this:

Hi there! My name is _____. I'm a Young Living essential oils distributor. Essential oils are used for cleaning, personal care products, supplements, to get chemicals out of the home, and to support systems in the body. What does that mean? I would never go a winter without RC in my diffuser during cold and flu season—it's wonderful for respiratory support. Peppermint is the first thing I apply when my stomach feels off—it's a digestive system support oil. Many people buy the kit for Pan Away alone. You will love it on your muscles! I started my Young Living journey with a starter kit. It's the best place to begin because it's the only thing on Young Living's site that's half off. Once you have a kit, every oil for life is 24 percent off. No membership fees. No yearly fee. It's the best choice I made for my family this year. Here's how to learn more...

BAM.

Then...

–make sure they have a tool. If you can afford it, depending on how big the vendor event is. I like to hand off flyers to everyone with information on how to order and my business card, and for some, my audio cd's. It's a lecture they can tune into in their car on the way home.

Now follow up. When you leave that event, look at every person who said they were interested in learning more and make contact with them. This is where the goldmine part comes in. See if they'll get two non-oilers to come with them to meet you for coffee or dinner—and you're off and running. You now have a new friend circle.

CHAPTER 13

KEYS TO CONFIDENCE

What are the reasons that you lack confidence? Nail down your root cause.

_____

_____

Did God make you that way?

_____

This is the fork in the road for you for this business. For you to be successful from here on out, you have a big decision to make. You have to decide that your desire to be successful is greater than your fear of failure. This is where you really have to make the decision that you want it. For some people, that decision, conscious and spoken aloud, is enough for them to move on and knock this out of the ballpark.

For others, it takes a bit more. The emotional abuse runs deep. The pain from the past is raw. The walls built around them are high. The experiences they have had lead them to believe they are not good, not worth it, not believable. The thing is, if you believe that about yourself, you emulate that to the people around you. And here's the thing: IT'S NOT TRUE. God made no mistakes when He made you. His plan is totally perfect. So you can stay where you are and keep believing lies, or you can take steps to get out from the place you have been living and fly. You were created to help other people. If you live in emotional bondage, you can't pour into anyone.

YOUR ASSIGNMENT: TAKE STEPS TOWARD CONFIDENCE

If you're in that place, do me a favor. Go to danijohnson.com and just look at one of her First Steps to Success seminars. It's a chunk of change for a weekend. But I've had dozens and dozens of my team members go through the training, and never once have any of them said it wasn't worth it financially. Please hear my heart, leader. This truly is not me trying to sell you something. I have absolutely nothing to gain from you going. But I am that confident that it will be a game changer for you emotionally. If your barrier is your confidence, this will be the best investment you make in your business. If you can't get people to attend your classes—and you have tried all my tips in this book—you NEED to get to Dani Johnson.

John's and my OGV was 46,000 when we first went. Five months later, it was 152,000. It's because she helps you get rid of the emotional baggage that's keep you from connecting with people. If you lack confidence, if you make excuses, if you are in a rut, if you have plateaued, if you can't get people to class, if you feel overwhelmed, you should be at her training. And you should get your leaders there. The more leaders you get there, the faster you will grow. I took 30 leaders my next Dani event and our OGV spiked to 185,000 this fall. Our pace is now 245,000 OGV before Christmas. If this is the turning point for you, write down the date you're going to Dani and make no excuses. Just get there.

Date I am going to Dani:_____

Current OGV: _____

Date I went to Dani: _____

OGV 6 months later: _____

If you think you have this business nailed on your own, it's time to start walking, talking, and thinking like a Diamond—and holding classes and training leaders like one. You were made to pour into the people around you. But you have to be in a place to pour. If you're always running on empty, it's time to figure out why and change it.

CHAPTER 14

YOUR BUSINESS TOOLKIT:
OILY TOOLS, TAXBOT, AND MORE

This is a very simple workbook chapter to write, because I want you to pick up the resources in this chapter and start to utilize them. They make everything else easier.

Oily Tools

Go to the app store, download it to your cell phone, and pay $7 a month for the program. It's genius. Not only can you see your paycheck projected by rank, you can also see your pace OGV (where the program believes you'll end up at the end of the month.) This has been one of the biggest motivators for me to keep going in my Young Living business. It's the best $7 dollars I spent outside my starter kit.

Taxbot.

Go online and pay for the program. It's $5 a month for Young Living distributors. You can track your mileage from your cell phone and it automatically uploads. It also connects with your bank and lets you know when receipts need to be scanned in for charges to be reconciled. It makes taxes easy. And that's saying a lot. You can get 50 percent off Taxbot each month ($5 instead of $10) by using this link: https://taxbot.com/z/yl/

While we are on the topic of paychecks and taxes, may I freely offer some advice? I am a big proponent on living on less then you make. Being a millionaire won't help you if you're spending more than a million dollars. John and I draw up a business budget every single month based on my checks. You can do this, too, if your check is 50 dollars or 50,000 dollars.

A family business typically in the United States doesn't see a profit until year seven. In Young Living, I saw a profit on month one. My very first paycheck was $340, twice what I spent on my starter kit. I paid my husband back for the kit, ordered business cards, and placed my Essential Rewards order with that first check, and stayed totally debt free. All you need to launch your business is a starter kit and a 101 Script.

When I first started, all the cash from my business went right back into my business. When I retired a year after I got my kit, I set aside a portion of my check for debt to cover what my anchoring income had covered, but most still went to my business. When my husband retires on Labor Day this year, 2 years out from getting our kit, then this outline will look a bit different. For the purpose of writing a starter kit to Silver book, most generally aren't retired yet and using their Young Living income for their personal finances. If you put it back into the business, it will grow your business. In Gameplan 2, look for our new budget, with our family finances mixed in.

This is how I delegate my paycheck right now. Our income is about $10,000 a month, but I base it on our lowest check over the past six months, $7,600. If I have extra, it goes to tithe, debt, or savings.

10% tithe	$760
20% taxes	$1520
20% debt	$1520
12% payroll	$912

(I pay my kids to help me at classes, and have a personal assistant to help with mailings. She works about 15 hours a month.) If you don't need this category, add it to debt

5% Essential Rewards	$380 (SWEET!)
15% gas and food	$1140

(I use this to get to classes, and also help with our budget)

10% Young Living expenses	$760

If you have a NingXia bar at classes, or order samples or flyers)

4% travel	$304
4% awards and recognition on my team	$304

That's what my business budget looks like right now. Each month my check changes, and I just adjust it to the ratios above. It works! I saved all the money for my taxes, gave generously, paid a lot of debt, had the income to visit and train and recognize leaders, and cover my essential rewards order.

ibloom

I seriously love this planner. I love it because it's Christ-focused, but also because it gives me ample room to write out goals. A man without a vision is lost. You must know where you're going to get there. This is just a great company with a lot of integrity, and I love to support them. All my top leaders get ibloom planners from me each year. It keeps them (and me) organized! To save a little cash, you can do the printable version and print it at home and put it in a binder.

Books.

Oh my. I could give you 100 different books to read. That's probably one of the top things I get asked by my team- "what are you reading this week,

Sarah?". About every other week someone asks me to post my current reading list, and it usually has at least 30 books on it. Since I'm used to reading 39 newspapers each morning to write news the past 18 years, I read a lot. I believe if you're not reading, you're not growing. It's a way to pour into you. If you are about to finish Gameplan and you truly want to keep growing in your network marketing awesomeness, I am working on a 7-week Rise to Silver bootcamp: Gameplan Edition that will kick your tush. It's 35 hours of intense videos and intimate training. You can do it on your own or in a small group. You'll be able to find it at oilabilityteam.com (This is only for over achievers!) I have also hinted that I'm working on a Gameplan II—which will be for Silvers and above.

If you want a little less work because frankly, this book knocked you flat out and set you into full-on adrenal fatigue, here are my favorite from-the-hammock reads:

- Eric Worre's Go Pro
- Eric Worre's Rise of the Entrepreneur DVD
- Dale Carnegie's How To Win Friends and Influence People
- My favorite book on aromatherapy is still Dr. David Stewart's Healing Oils of the Bible.
- The Essential Oil Truth Second Edition: the Facts Without the Hype by Jen O'Sullivan
- French Aromatherapy: Essential Oil Recipes & Usage Guide by Jen O'Sullivan
- Living Balanced: Healthy Mind & Body Reference Guide by Stacey Kimbrell

Just remember: don't get so caught up in learning and education that you're not out there teaching classes. When your classes suffer, it's time to cut back. I pretty much only read when I cannot do anything else: when I'm in an airplane, when I'm in a hotel, when I'm waiting for a kid to get out of Boy Scouts or ballet.

YOUR ASSIGNMENT: GET YOUR TOOLS

This is a four part assignment, covering each of the key areas of a well-organized business.

1. If you love reading and want to continue to grow, make a list of 3 books you'd like to check out yourself, pick a copy up and have at it.

   ☐ _____

   ☐ _____

   ☐ _____

2. Draw up a rough draft of your budget, where you'd like to see your pennies go from this business. Then for 30 days, track all your spending and see where it goes. See if you can stick to the percentages you have written down.

My Young Living Budget:

_____ %	_____
_____ %	_____
_____ %	_____
_____ %	_____
_____ %	_____
_____ %	_____
_____ %	_____
_____ %	_____
_____ %	_____
_____ %	_____

3. Pick up a planner and start using it. Track your mileage. Write down your classes. Prep for next month.

4. At least check out Taxbot and Oily Tools. Purchase them when you see you have the money in your business budget. You'll be glad you did.

CHAPTER 15

GROWING YOUR BUSINESS THROUGH BLOGGING

This is the only chapter that you get a get-out-of-jail-for-free pass. If you truly are not a writer, you can skip the blogging advice and I promise I will not hunt you down. The dog has eaten your homework and you are forgiven.

There are those of you who believe you have a writing talent, but truly, your writing is depressing. It's ok. I am not good at Math. You really don't want to see me doing Calculus—I get to the point where I'm throwing the book at the wall. If you think you have talent but everyone around you says it's just not so, you, too, may skip this chapter. In fact, please skip it. I am asking in the name of all the people out there who do technical editing for a living.

If you want some quick tips for making social media an asset to your business (even without blogging!) then don't skip this chapter!

For the Bloggers

If you are in the minority that have both the writing skills and technical aptitude, go ahead and give blogging a try. I'd encourage you to go to Wordpress and try knocking out your own blog. Get 10 posts up before you make it live so there is some content on the sight.

These are the steps to launching a blog:

1. Choose a name
2. Choose a hosting company
3. Choose a domain name (ours is oilabilityteam.com)
4. Choose a logo
5. Set up your page on Wordpress

And you are off and running!

YOUR ASSIGNMENT: UPDATE YOUR SOCIAL MEDIA PROFILES

You may never be a blogger, but I bet you have a Facebook profile, an Instagram identity, or Twitter account! Make sure people who already follow you know that you love the oils and that you can help educate them. For those of us that truly have no talent to create a blog or website, you can still have a rockstar social media presence. Start with whatever platforms you're already on.

1. Update your profile to include that you are with Young Living.

2. Use the tips in Chapter 15 to share short, enthusiastic, compliant posts alongside whatever else you share online.

Don't hide the fact that you're an oiler. People do business with those they know, like and trust. They may be interested in oils, but want to learn from a friend—and that friend could be you! I have sold two kits simply by people checking out my profiles. We can share oils online just by putting 140 characters onto Twitter about our son's stinky shoes. It's possible! So start there.

And if you have no gift, stay far, far away from Wordpress.

Let me repeat that: far away. It falls under the 'distractions' category for you.

CHAPTER 16

STAYING LEGAL: COMPREHENSIVE FDA TRAINING

Write down 10 things you're not allowed to do:

1) _____

2) _____

3) _____

4) _____

5) _____

6) _____

7) _____

8) _____

9) _____

10 _____

I tell people if you're not sure if it's legal, just think of what is on the shelves at Walgreens. If an item is sold in that store, it's likely FDA approved. You can't talk about your oils like you would about any item at a drug store. That means no bug spray or sunscreen. It also means the FDA is looking for intent. You can't market "sun spray"—or they'll be on to you. Run your business with integrity. Let people do their own research on the oils. Don't make things up illicitly and don't try to skirt around the rules.

Why does the FDA put limits on what you can say about oils? _____

_____

_____

Why doesn't Young Living just become FDA approved? You tell me below.

_____

_____

_____

_____

YOUR ASSIGNMENT: EQUIP, DON'T PRESCRIBE

The moral of the chapter: teach people how to fish instead of giving them fish. What are some resources you can give them to start their own research? List 2.

_____

_____

CHAPTER 17

THE YOUNG LIVING COMPENSATION PLAN, IN LAYMAN'S TERMS

This is where it gets tricky! Who REALLY understands the comp plan? I have a little secret for you. You don't need to. It's completely broken down for you in the Virtual Office under "my account". Just look up your commissions check, click on each item (Unilevel, starter kit bonuses, etc.), and you can see exactly who you were paid on, and how much. It's actually quite fun to see it all broken down.

It's not bad to have a basic understanding though. Tell me what each of the 4 things below are:

Starter Kit bonuses: _____

_____

Fast Start: _____

_____

Unilevel: _____

_____

Rising Star and Generation Leadership Bonuses: _____

_____

On what day of the month are you paid? _____

Now write down a goal. What do you want your paycheck to be 6 months from now? _____

This may sound a little silly, but it really helps to visualize where you want to be. I want you to take a check out of your checkbook, sign Mary Young's name to it, and fill it out for where you'd like to see your Young Living monthly paycheck—one year from today. Then tape it right in this workbook under this paragraph. When you hit benchmarks, write them down next to the check, and the date you hit it. It's incredible the places you will go when you can see in your head where you want to end up. It's like following the basketball as you throw it through the air, or watching the hoop where you want it to go. It's much more likely to go in if your eyes are on the hoop. Fill out a check, tape in on this page, and keep your eyes on the hoop.

What rank do you want to be THIS YEAR? _____

Let's break it down into smaller goals to help you get to that paycheck. For me, John and I have a goal of Diamond. We're about 100,000 OGV down and 2 of our 5 legs are about 5-thousand OGV short. So my goals look like this:

Month 1: Increase 2 legs OGV by 1500 each, to 11,500

25,000 OGV growth

Month 2: Increase 2 legs OGV by 1500 each, to 13,000

25,000 OGV growth

Month 3: Increase 2 legs OGV by 1500 each, to 14,500

25,000 OGV growth

Month 4: Increase 2 legs the last 500

25,000 OGV growth

Now what do I need to do to attain those goals? First, I need to be strategic. I may be getting requests to teach on my other 3 legs, but for a season, I have to laser hone in on the two legs that are too low to rank. So for 4 months, all of my classes must be under a person on one of those two legs. I won't get distracted. I focus solely on them to get to the goal.

What about OGV growth? 25,000 OGV is a lot to grow in 1 month, even for a Platinum. How do I attain that? My husband and I did some brainstorming on how to grow OGV, and we leaned on the wisdom of the Diamonds before us. I asked the what worked and what didn't work. I got a few tips.

How to Increase OGV

Get as many people as you can to convention (so we incentivized our team with swag bags and got 30 people there this year, 10 times more than last year)

Get as many people as you can to Dani Johnson training to get rid of emotional blocks holding them back from ranking (we were able to get 27 people there this year)

Do a Silver bootcamp. I recommend the resources at oilabilityteam.com. Do you know the Gameplan book and workbook were designed to be used in a small group format? You can go on Facebook Live or Zoom and take a chapter a week and do it with your leaders. At that rate, with 24 chapters, it would either take you 6 months, or you could meet for 30 minutes a night for 24 straight days and do a 5-week bootcamp. Option 3 is to simply take the 3-page leader training in the back of Gameplan and break it out into a week of intense training with vision boards, the Rise of the Entrepreneur DVD, and accountability and incentives.

Consider contests and awards. Our team goes CRAZY for them. We do them within our budget, but we have something special set aside each month, even if it's just an hour of coaching with me.

Launch a Facebook page where everyone in the business can grow together and are on the same page for encouragement and leadership.

Do a weekly Facebook live or Zoom chat for leadership training.

To increase our OGV by 100,000, our team needs to sell 1,000 kits. If I break that over 4 months, that's 250 kits a month. Our average team wide is 200 kits a month. I'm setting a goal of 250 kits a month plus 30 new people on Essential Rewards to maintain the volume. I'll give awards for kit sales or Essential Rewards sign ups.

Do you see how I laid out tangible, doable goals?

Let's walk you through process now, so you can work on ranking yourself.

YOUR ASSIGNMENT: MAKE SPECIFIC GOALS

What is your desired rank? _____

How many months do you want to take to get there? _____

What do you have to do for OGV and for your legs to attain that rank?

_____

_____

What tactics do you think will work to specifically increase OGV and work on those legs? _____

_____

_____

Make a list of goals you can work on each month to get where you want to be:

Month 1: _____

Month 2: _____

Month 3: _____

Month 4: _____

Month 5: _____

Month 6: _____

Here's one word of caution. Be diligent. And be focused. If you lose your focus, you'll lose your goal. Lay boundaries while you're working on rank, and stick closely with the goals you have laid out. And you will get there.

CHAPTER 18

A Young Living Strategy Guide On Where to Sign New Oilers

Explain to me the strategy of where to sign people. When you are just starting, what should you do? _____

_____

Sponsor and enroller. Who is the higher rank? _____

What is PGV—and why does it matter so much at the start of your business?

_____

_____

Is it better to work on PGV now or later? _____

_____

Why is it smart to build under your leaders, instead of signing everyone under you (once you have your 1000 PGV)? _____

_____

Let's talk about blaming others for challenges in your business. Do you have a grass-is-greener-on-the-other-side mentality? _____

_____

What do you need to do to succeed at this? _____

_____

Who is responsible for your Young Living business? _____

Let's play the fill in the blank game again, and see if you can keep up with the strategy in this chapter.

Don't underestimate _____

Only think _____ legs ahead.

Why?? _____

Ratios. Start by teaching _____

70% of people who come to make and takes _____

If you see a little plus sign next to their name _____

_____

What is sponsor? _____

What is enroller?_____

Can you be the sponsor for someone under you? _____

Why? _____

_____

How can you remember which is which? E comes before _____

YOUR ASSIGNMENT: IDENTIFY YOUR LEGS

Write down the names of 2 people you think may have the potential to be business builders:

As a backup, write down the names of 2 people you believe would order 100PV a month, or you'd just truly like to see blessed:

This week... talk to them.

_____

_____

CHAPTER 19

THE KEY TO REACHING AND MAINTAINING RANK

Can you wait until you're a Silver to start signing people up for Essential Rewards? _____

Tell me why. _____

_____

_____

YOUR ASSIGNMENT: CREATE YOUR ESSENTIAL REWARDS PACKAGE

Each person has a different system to putting together mailings (or "care packages")—for their new members. Take a photo of one of your care packages and tape it right here—in this book. It'll give you a giggle in 2 or 3 years as you get better and better with them, to see the things you included when you first began. When I first started, it was usually a business card and a flyer. Now it's Cool Azul pain cream, a sample of Thieves cleaner, or something very practical that they can try out. I also love to give my audio lectures on CD to them, to start to train them how important it is to use oils over chemicals.

Place your photo here:

Whatever you decide to include, each package must have a purpose. It needs to explain Essential Rewards, or no one will be signing up for ER. They need to have ideas of what to order, because they're entirely new to oils. They need to understand the promos for that month, because they likely will spend a bit more to hit a benchmark. So every package I send out at least has those 3 items in it, plus a few extras.

CHAPTER 20

BALANCING THE BUSINESS, SETTING BOUNDARIES, AND TREATING YOUR BUSINESS AS A BUSINESS

Are you an overscheduler?

If you are not, you have permission to skip this chapter too. (Look at that! I gave a free pass for 2 chapters!!!) If you are, I have yet another reading list for you. (After this workbook, of course!) These are my favorite reads for how to balance the business alongside your own life. You don't want your kids eating cereal and apples and cheese for six months while you build to Silver, and you don't want it to take 18 years to rank, so how do you do it all? How do you fit it in one 24-hour day?

These were the books I digested. Order them and put a check mark next to them as you finish them. You must learn to manage your time wisely. I assure you—it can be done. It just takes self-control and discipline.

- ☐ Start with Dani's training series on time management, Time Secrets.
- ☐ Lisa Terkeursts' "The Best Yes"
- ☐ Dr. Henry Cloud and Dr. John Townsend's "Boundaries"

As you wait for those to arrive, there are a few practical things we can do to help you lay out a Gameplan for how to get Young Living in your day.

Budget your day out.

Literally.

Take the next few lines, and write out when you'd set aside time to do your business. Leave time for follow up, mailings, and leadership training. Then pop in some classes, too. And let's see what the layout of your week would look like.

MONDAY

7:00am
8:00am
9:00am
10:00am
11:00am
12:00pm
1:00pm
2:00pm
3:00pm
4:00pm
5:00pm
6:00pm
7:00pm
8:00pm
9:00pm

TUESDAY

7:00am
8:00am
9:00am
10:00am
11:00am
12:00pm
1:00pm
2:00pm
3:00pm
4:00pm
5:00pm
6:00pm
7:00pm
8:00pm
9:00pm

WEDNESDAY

7:00am
8:00am
9:00am
10:00am
11:00am
12:00pm
1:00pm
2:00pm
3:00pm
4:00pm
5:00pm
6:00pm
7:00pm
8:00pm
9:00pm

THURSDAY

7:00am
8:00am
9:00am
10:00am
11:00am
12:00pm
1:00pm
2:00pm
3:00pm
4:00pm
5:00pm
6:00pm
7:00pm
8:00pm
9:00pm

FRIDAY

7:00am
8:00am
9:00am
10:00am
11:00am
12:00pm
1:00pm
2:00pm
3:00pm
4:00pm
5:00pm
6:00pm
7:00pm
8:00pm
9:00pm

SATURDAY

7:00am
8:00am
9:00am
10:00am
11:00am
12:00pm
1:00pm
2:00pm
3:00pm
4:00pm
5:00pm
6:00pm
7:00pm
8:00pm
9:00pm

Now do it. Hold yourself to a clock and make it happen. Cut out the distractions sucking your time from accomplishing your goal. If you have a goal of 1 hour a day, make it happen. If it's 30 minutes, that's 30 minutes you're not spending right now. It all comes down to your diligence. You have to stop when the clock switches to the next hour. Make sure your priorities are in line, and you've got time set aside for the things that matter most.

If you are a homeschooler, or if you just need some more balance to keep your home clean and you have a couple of kids, there was a wonderful book (with charts to fill in and hang on the wall) that I use a lot in my home. You can find it at titus2ministries.com

Look for: "Managers of their Chores". "Managers of their Homes" is also good. A second resources is the Accountable Kids set if you are having a hard time getting your kids to help you out with the house. Find info on that at accountablekids.com

As for "Managers of their Chores", I use the same charts in that book to lay out my day. It's literally just a grid, broken into 30 minute or 1 hour increments. And it works!

Now when it comes time to actually fill that hour of business time with work, what do you do?

One of the downsides to running your own business is that the work is never finished. You never get to a place where you feel like you've arrived and you can just walk away. In news, once I shut off my mic, I went home and didn't think about news for about 18 hours. It was wonderful. I was fully engaged in homeschooling. But with a home-based business, you always have a to-do list.

How do you get around the always-behind feeling? Shorten your list. Make it manageable. I'm going to tell you about a simple exercise you can do right when you wake up—one that will get more and more practical as your team grows—because I'll tell you, managing 3200 people can take a lot out of you some days! You bounce from leader to leader and fire to fire on some days, and excitement and joy and jubilation in 40 places other days. Time management is critical the larger you grow!

As you rise, think about your day—and what the absolutely most important things of your business are. It may be helping a member move someone by a deadline, or changing someone's Essential Reward's order before it goes through, or setting up your classes so you can market them for the next 2 weeks. Whatever the 3 most important things are, those go on your list—and you don't beat yourself up if you feel there are 5 more things that should go on it, but that you never get to.

Put those items in order of importance. And I don't do anything else (during your business work time) until those items are done first.

Our Diamond, Jay Carter, has a slightly different approach. He actually makes a list of 7 things—but it includes personal items like working out, getting in the Word, and making food or cleaning. After 7 items, his day is done and he has the liberty to rest. It's wonderful.

YOUR ASSIGNMENT: MAKE YOUR LIST OF THREE

Starting today–right now–make a list of the three things you'd like to do today. And keep the list manageable—if you only have an hour, don't write "read the whole Gameplan book."

1) _____

2) _____

3) _____

Try those tactics when budgeting out your work day.

Treat each day as a true work day, too. When I am getting ready to work on Young Living business, I will change out of my sweatpants. I may put a little makeup on.

I set aside time and the kids know they are not to interrupt me—it's the same as if I'm in the anchor chair. It's my time. They use that time to work quietly on their work or their readers, or they get extra chores. Establish a sense of importance around the family business. But when it's time to shut it off, focus on them.

Have an end time each day, so your kids know it's not all-consuming. When we are homeschooling, my phone is shut off. They have all my attention. When we're outside playing laser tag as a family, I'm not taking business calls. I have set business hours that are respected both by my team and by my family. And family time is respected by John and I. No business.

Try sticking to your business schedule this week and see how much you accomplish and how balanced you feel!

CHAPTER 21

FINDING AND RAISING LEADERS

This is probably the simplest chapter to write for the workbook. I want you to go to the Appendix in Gameplan, grab the "Teacher Training: How to Launch Yong Living Leaders" section, and get in front of a mirror and read it. Then go practice it on your mom.

Then every time you see a little plus sign in your organization next to a name in "my organization" in the Virtual Office, it means someone has sold a kit. They need to be trained. In month 2 of my business, I had 27 different people share a kit. Most of them have now dropped off my team because I never took the time to train them on how to get their oils for free. Take that 3-page training and get in front of them over lunch or dinner, and have some one-on-one time. Show them where this goes. Every plus sign is a potential leader.

Some people may just want free oils. They truly have no desire to do a Young Living business. In fact, according to statistics, 92 percent of Young Living distributors are users only. That boggles my mind! Even if your goal isn't to get a generous income, you can get your oils for free with so little effort! One class a month, a 2-hour time commitment a month, would cut it. So if that's their first goal, that's a good place to start. (Though after that first class I'd still put a copy of Gameplan in their hands to help them see the vision of where this goes!)

What does getting your oils for free look like? One class a month, until you have 10 people solidly on Essential Rewards. Ten people under you on ER is enough to get a decent check to pay NingXia for the family or restock your laundry and dish soap. It's very doable.

YOUR ASSIGNMENT: PRACTICE THE TEACHER TRAINING

Your only homework assignment for this chapter is to practice the Teacher Training script and start training your leaders. It's a simple process. Read the 3-page leaders script and give them a tour of the virtual office in person. Make sure you go over the "Rank Qualification" button so they understand what they need to do to rank up. That's it. Then have them do the seven assignments to earn a copy of Gameplan and they are off and running, through one cycle of their Young Living business. And you have a business builder that is lightening your load.

You can teach one class on a Saturday. But if you have 10 leaders doing the same thing, you just taught 11 classes. And that, my friend, is the entire secret to the chessboard of network marketing. Multiply yourself.

CHAPTER 22

HOW TO PRAY OVER YOUR YOUNG LIVING BUSINESS

This chapter is a bit more hands on. This is probably the most overlooked thing in your entire business. God says that when we come to Him, He is faithful to hear our prayers. He wants abundance for His kids. The trouble is, we never come to Him. And worse yet, when we do, we pray very generic prayers.

I started a habit of praying before each class, publicly, with my team leaders before I taught, from the very first class. I really believe pre-class prayer time with my leaders, plus a prayer journal, as well as collective prayers on our team have been the catapult that exploded our business. Your work means nothing if you do not have favor. You have no favor if you do not ask.

I have a pretty straightforward system for praying, because my memory is atrocious. I went out and bought a little journal. I divided each page into 3 columns: thanks, leaders, goals.

Thanks is just a list of all the amazing things I see God doing. It's something that worked out great. A deal we got on a projector. Unexplained income. A visit from a new, energetic leader. The things I'm grateful for. I like to call them Godwinks.

Leaders are specific prayers for my team. They are the things that are posted and unposted. They are the texts, the stalking I do on their personal pages, the precious nuggets they share from their own lives. I pray diligently and specifically over each of them. I pray for rank. I pray for their families. I pray for OGV. I pray for their burdens. And we lift each other up.

Goals are for my business. I mentioned them earlier: a 100,000 OGV spike. 25,000 a month, 2 legs built to 15,000. I write very specific goals down, then my husband and I pray collectively over them.

One more thing... as you do this—leave a little space to the left of each line. Go through your journal once a week and check off the prayers that were answered. I even like to put a date next to it. It will blow your mind how many prayers God truly answers for us. We just don't pay attention!

YOUR ASSIGNMENT: START A PRAYER JOURNAL

Get a Notebook. Make your columns. Start writing things down. Start praying. BAM. You can practice today by filling in the lines below with 5 Thanks, 5 prayers for your leaders, and 5 business goals.

Also: go rent the movie "The War Room" and watch it. If you are overwhelmed or feel weird about praying, that movie will help tremendously.

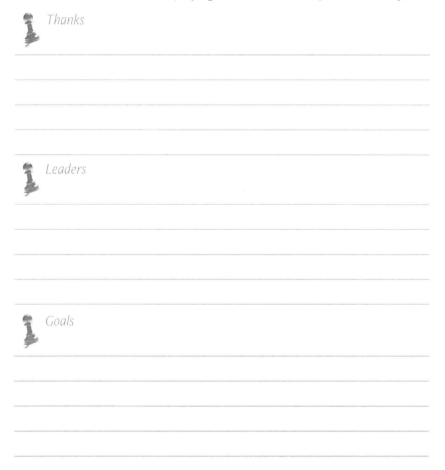

Thanks

_____

_____

_____

Leaders

_____

_____

_____

Goals

_____

_____

_____

_____

CHAPTER 23

AVOIDING DISTRACTIONS

Hear my heart on this chapter closely, leader. These things can DESTROY your business. They can take your growth to such a snail's pace that you begin to believe that network marketing doesn't work. It does work. But you have to invest time in areas that make it grow. If you sit around doing make and takes, and statistics show 70% of people never make the product again or order the oils, how does that raise leaders or sell starter kits? You are walking down a dead-end street. Invest in areas that grow. You wouldn't put $1000 in the stock market knowing you'd lose 70%. Why do you spend time in areas that don't grow your business?

Take a few moments and write down the top distractions I see among business builders.

Now be honest. Do you fall into any of these categories? Tell me where you stumble.

Tell me what you can do to change that.

YOUR ASSIGNMENT: FOCUS ON GROWTH

Make a list of what you need to do to grow, and stick to the list. (Hint, hint: hold classes, train leaders, do follow up to get people on Essential Rewards! Write only those 3 things on the lines below.) Every time you are doing a task, ask yourself if it falls under one of those three categories. If it doesn't, why are you wasting your time? If you plateau, open your workbook back to this page and look at the lines below. Hold yourself accountable for how you are spending your time.

_____

_____

_____

_____

_____

_____

_____

Don't fall into the pitfall of wasting time on things that don't grow your business. This truly is simple. Grab the 101 Script and get it in front of as many people as you can, however you are gifted to do that. Train leaders. Contact the people you meet in classes or that get kits. That's it. If you're doing anything outside that, and it's slowing or stopping your ability to teach, your attention is in the wrong place.

CHAPTER 24

ENCOURAGEMENT FOR THE CLIMB

Do you find that you're always looking around you? Looking at other people's rank, wondering why you haven't grown as fast as that girl that signed up the same time you did, wondering why that person signed on that other person's team.

It doesn't matter.

This is a tool that the evil one uses to bait you into giving up. Here's the thing: you write your own story. You craft what you want the outcome to be. If you do it fast, great. If you do it slow, there's nothing wrong with that!

Spend so much time teaching classes and raising leaders that you don't have the time to worry about the muck and the drama around you. Don't look into other's organizations, just look into your own. Be less distracted. Take your business seriously.

YOUR ASSIGNMENT: FOCUS ON WHAT SUCCESS LOOKS LIKE FOR YOU

Take a moment write down what your perfect day would look like. How would you spend your time? What would you do for hobbies? Who would you pour into? Write it down as if it's tomorrow. That's the day you're going for. Don't look at other people's days, focus on yours. And get there. When you are discouraged, come read your perfect day again, envision it in your mind, and go out and schedule a class.

Now I want you to take the Gameplan challenge in this chapter. Sit down and write out your vision. Write down your goals. Make a Gameplan. Open your calendar and schedule a class. Ask three people to invite to it. Don't just say you'll do it or think you'll do it—make it happen. Set a date for your next class TODAY.

The date of that class is: _____

CHAPTER 25

CHEAT SHEET TO GO FROM STARTER KIT TO SILVER

You just finished this whole book. (Make sure you check out the Workbook Appendixes, they are gold too! There is a special Appendix just for you guys!)

Now what do you do? Apply it! If you can't remember want a quick overview of your personal Gameplan, here's a 1-page cheat sheet. As you complete each item, check it off below. Write the date you did it. And hold yourself accountable to the Gameplan book. You control the pace of your way out. It's time to fight for your future.

Order your premium starter kit online (use my number, 1879195, if you have no team.)

Photocopy Appendix A, the Simple 101 Script, from the back of this book and read it.

Make a list of all of your contacts EVERYWHERE. Grab them off Facebook, your Christmas card list, and even former co-workers.

Set up a Facebook event for a class. (Click on "more" then "events" to get to the page). Fill out the description. Use powerful verbs and make the lecture exciting. Put a photo on your event.

Ask 3 people off that list to invite 50 of their friends to the class. They can't just share it to their page, they have go under the "invite friends" button in the event and invite people. Ask them to say something nice about you and the class.

Market the class for 2-3 weeks, no more then 1-2 posts a day.

Open your doors and read that script to the people sitting on your coach. End with a strong close. Tell them where to get the starter kit.

Do good follow up. Call or mail a hand-written note to those that came. (I don't do this by email, it's too impersonal.) Stay in contact. The average person can only say no 7 times.

Rinse and repeat. Teach 4-6 classes a month to aim for Silver in Six. As someone on your team turns to the person next to them and sells their own kit, grab the Teacher Training and train them. Show them "rank qualification" on the Virtual office. Keep in contact with them once a week. Build under two strong leaders to get to silver. When your OGV crosses 10,000 and each leg is over 4,000, you have made it.

Don't hunt people. Don't get lost in the no's. (There will be far more no's then yes's—that's the nature of this business!) Change the philosophy of how you see the business. You are collecting relationships, not starter kits. Don't take it personally when they don't order. Move on, and keep yourself so busy scheduling classes that you don't notice the no's.

Pray. Pray over your business and use Abundance oil abundantly. God has you, and God has this. You were meant to be free. Go out there, world changer. Be bold. Have confidence. And bless all those you meet.

Fill out the Accountability Worksheet in this workbook. (There is also the same form in the Gameplan book). Fill it out every single month to keep you on track. It works!

YOUR ASSIGNMENT: CREATE YOUR PORTABLE OFFICE

Practice putting together your portable office. Grab some small organza bags, a 101 DVD or audio cd, stuff it with flyers and business cards and samples. Carry a few of them with you everywhere and hand them out when you strike up a good conversation. It's a great supplement to classes because it's a portable class. They can listen to an audio cd in their car, and touch base with you afterward.

Put these habits into practice and it will establish trends for you to grow your team.

Practice follow up

Each time someone gets a kit, or expresses interest in a kit, make sure you're sending hand written notes, picking up the phone and calling them, or talking to them in person. Get into the practice of staying in touch with your team.

Raise the level of your own leadership

I don't believe in leadership training that paralyzes you—training where you don't move on your own business. But you've seen a few of my favorite books. I'll add more below. Get them on audio book and spend 15 minutes a day in the car, listening. Grow yourself.

Some of my favs:

- [ ] Gameplan on audio cd—listen to it as you drive every 6 months to regain your focus
- [ ] Gameplan workbook + book set; start a 24 week Gameplan Silver Bootcamp with your own team using these resources. Read a chapter from the book and do a workbook chapter together once a week. If your team is too large to get in a room, do it on Zoom or Facebook Live. (There are bundle discounts for leaders! Check it out at oilabilityteam. com)
- [ ] Robert Kiyosaki Rich Dad, Poor Dad
- [ ] Anything by Jim Rohn
- [ ] Anything by Dani Johnson
- [ ] Anything by Richard Bliss Brook
- [ ] Anything from Eric Worre
- [ ] Monique McClean's Circle of Success
- [ ] Adam Green's 25 to Life: Jailbreak Your 9 to 5
- [ ] Jake Dempsey's Driven for Success: Road Map to the Comp Plan
- [ ] Steve Sheridan's Journey To Health and Wealth
- [ ] The Four Year Career, Young Living Edition

Raise your leaders

Make it a point to connect with your leaders every week. Know how to pray for them. Work with them gently on their weaknesses.

Run your business like a business

Have set business hours. Write them down and stick to them. It works. Even if you can commit only 15 minutes a day, that will make a difference in how you grow.

Schedule your classes at least 2-4 weeks in advance. When I get to the last week of the month, I'll set up Facebook events for the next month's classes. Always stay a month ahead so people know where you are and can commit to coming.

Have fun

Your leaders won't want to do this if they see you working yourself to the bone. I recently flew to Alaska to teach four classes in the Fairbanks area. I took Sunday off to hike with my team, do some whitewater rafting, and soak it all in. There is more to this business then follow up and classes! There are relationships. Don't get so caught up in the sale that you lose best part: those around you.

You have survived the Gameplan Workbook! Congratulations! There are a couple of incredible resources in the Appendix to this book too, so go check them out! And keep an eye out for Gameplan 2, because you'll need it once you hit Silver!

Happy oiling!

OIL ABILITY GAMEPLAN ACCOUNTABILITY WORKSHEET

"A dream is just a dream. A goal is a dream with a plan and a deadline." -Harvey MacKay

"A goal without a plan is just a wish." -Anonymous

"Setting goals is the first step in turning the invisible to visible." -Tony Robbins

"People with goals succeed because they know where they are going." -Earl Nightingale

"The plans of the diligent lead to profit as surely as haste leads to poverty." Proverbs 21:5

OIL ABILITY GAMEPLAN ACCOUNTABILITY WORKSHEET

Rules: find a partner, fill it out by the 25th each month, and touch base once a week.

There are only 3 things that grow your business: holding classes, doing follow up, and raising leaders. This chart hones in on those 3 things and helps you set tangible goals and keeps you accountable.

Part 1: Classes

1) Schedule 4-6 classes for the month of: _____

2) Dates of classes scheduled (place a checkmark next to the class if you have set up a Facebook event and asked 3 people to invite 50 different people to it. This should be done before the end of the month so there is time to market classes early in the month.)

Class 1: _____ ☐
Class 2: _____ ☐
Class 3: _____ ☐
Class 4: _____ ☐
Class 5: _____ ☐
Class 6: _____ ☐

3) Overwhelmed by this schedule? A class a week is a commitment of 2 hours a week. That's 8 hours a month. You are giving 160 hours a month to a full time job. This is the job that gets you out of that job. Commit to at least one class a

week to grow fast enough that you'll stick with your Young Living business.

Part 2: Business Benchmark Wish List For This Month

OGV growth:_____

Leg growth:

    Leg 1: _____

    Leg 2: _____

This month I am focusing on these legs:_____

This month I am working with these leaders: _____
_____

(write their names and the dates you connected)

Name: _____

Dates: _____ , _____ , _____ , _____

Name: _____

Dates: _____ , _____ , _____ , _____

Name: _____

Dates: _____ , _____ , _____ , _____

Name: _____

Dates: _____ , _____ , _____ , _____

Make sure your leaders get this sheet and also have an accountability partner! Check in with them!

Part 3: Raising Leaders

Write a specific goal on the next sheet for at least two leaders. You should be connecting with your leaders once a week, via phone, text, Facebook, zoom, etc. Tangible goals might be:

- getting the Gameplan book in their hands,
- adding them to your business' Facebook page.
- coming up with a plan to get to convention
- giving them resources like flyers, books, DVD's or CD's
- helping them to teach their first 101 class
- watching them teach a class
- co-teaching a class
- training them to do online classes,
- coaching through their weaknesses

- going through the Teacher Training
- walking them through a Virtual Office tour

- _____

- _____

- _____

Part 4: Follow Up Goals

After each class or Teacher Training, have a plan for following up. For each person that came to class, I make a list of their names and text, call or email them. For each person that got a kit, I mail the package below. For each business builder, I mail the package below. On the back of this sheet, track your mailings.

Sarah's post-class plan (if they get a kit): a Welcome to Young Living book, a Thieves or NingXia flyer, an explanation of Essential Rewards and a list of the Essential Rewards freebies for the month, a DVD or 101 audio CD.

Sarah's post-Teacher Training follow up: the 101 Script in a manilla folder with instructions on how to teach (get 3 people on your couch, read the script, give them your distributor number as sponsor and enroller, rinse and repeat); the Teacher Training in a manilla folder to train them how to raise leaders, the Gameplan book, and links for them to plug in to your team's facebook page and online leadership trainings.

Part 5: Have Set Business Hours

This may not be possible if you have a shift with hours that change, but commit to a certain number of hours worked per week, connecting with leaders, marketing your classes, following up, doing mailings, and teaching classes. Even if you start with 1 hour a week, it's better than no commitment.

Week 1: _____

Week 2: _____

Week 3: _____

Week 4: _____

My best success this month was:

_____

_____

One area I can grow:

_____

_____

My 3-month OGV growth plan:

_____

_____

_____

People that are on my radar (for kits or as leaders):

_____

_____

_____

Congratulations! You made it to the end of the month! Time to start a new accountability sheet!

APPENDIX B

IDEAS FOR GETTING PEOPLE ON ESSENTIAL REWARDS

This is a special little nugget that we put together for all of you dedicated workbook users! You can download the full color images online at www.oilabilityteam.com

Tour of Young Living on 50 PV a month with Essential Rewards

Balance and Grow $69.50

Essential Rewards Points Earned 6.95 months 1-3, 13.90 months 4-24, 17.38 months 25+

Tour of Young Living on 50 PV a month with Essential Rewards

Chef Young Living $56.00

Essential Rewards Points Earned 5.60 months 1-3, 11.20 months 4-24, 14.00 months 25+

Tour of Young Living on 50 PV a month with Essential Rewards

Conquer Emotions $51.50

Essential Rewards Points Earned 5.15 months 1-3, 10.30 months 4-24, 12.88 months 25+

Tour of Young Living on 50 PV a month with Essential Rewards

Detox Your Body $59.25

Essential Rewards Points Earned 5.93 months 1-3, 11.85 months 4-24, 14.81 months 25+

Tour of Young Living on 50 PV a month with Essential Rewards

For the Kids $60.75

Essential Rewards Points Earned 6.08 months 1-3, 12.15 months 4-24, 15.19 months 25+

Tour of Young Living on 50 PV a month with Essential Rewards

Frankie Says Relax $54.25

Essential Rewards Points Earned 5.43 months 1-3, 10.85 months 4-24, 13.56 months 25+

Tour of Young Living on 50 PV a month with Essential Rewards

Oil Ability

Get Cleaning $50.75

Essential Rewards Points Earned 5.08 months 1-3, 10.15 months 4-24, 12.69 months 25+

Tour of Young Living on 50 PV a month with Essential Rewards

Oil Ability

Intro to Supplements $57.50

Essential Rewards Points Earned 5.75 months 1-3, 11.50 months 4-24, 14.38 months 25+

Tour of Young Living on 50 PV a month with Essential Rewards

Oil Ability

Old MacDonald Had a Farm $64.50

Essential Rewards Points Earned 5.70 months 1-3, 11.40 months 4-24, 14.25 months 25+

Tour of Young Living on 50 PV a month with Essential Rewards

Oil Ability

Oral Care $50.00

Essential Rewards Points Earned 5.00 months 1-3, 10.00 months 4-24, 12.50 months 25+

Tour of Young Living on 50 PV a month with Essential Rewards

Oil Ability

Personal Care $50.50

Essential Rewards Points Earned 5.05 months 1-3, 10.10 months 4-24, 12.63 months 25+

Tour of Young Living on 50 PV a month with Essential Rewards

Oil Ability

Rock Your Body $52.00

Essential Rewards Points Earned 5.20 months 1-3, 10.40 months 4-24, 13.00 months 25+

Tour of Young Living on 190 PV a month with Essential Rewards

Oil Ability

The Complete Bathroom Kit= $192.25

Essential Rewards Points Earned 19.23 months 1-3, 38.45 months 4-24, 48.06 months 25+
Plus all the free oils on the 190PV Level of Essential Rewards Freebies.

Tour of Young Living on 190 PV a month with Essential Rewards

Chemical Free Kids=$205.25

Essential Rewards Points Earned 20.53 months 1-3, 41.05 months 4-24, 51.31 months 25+
Plus all the free oils on the 190PV Level of Essential Rewards Freebies.

Tour of Young Living on 190 PV a month with Essential Rewards

Energy=$201.75

Essential Rewards Points Earned 20.18 months 1-3, 40.35 months 4-24, 50.44 months 25+
Plus all the free oils on the 190PV Level of Essential Rewards Freebies.

Tour of Young Living on 190 PV a month with Essential Rewards

For Little Noses=$240.25

Essential Rewards Points Earned 19.45 months 1-3, 38.90 months 4-24, 48.63 months 25+
Plus all the free oils on the 190PV Level of Essential Rewards Freebies.

Tour of Young Living on 190 PV a month with Essential Rewards

For Your Four-Legged Family Member=$269.00

Essential Rewards Points Earned 19.75 months 1-3, 39.50 months 4-24, 49.38 months 25+
Plus all the free oils on the 190PV Level of Essential Rewards Freebies.

Tour of Young Living on 190 PV a month with Essential Rewards

Just Breathe=$276.50

Essential Rewards Points Earned 19.20 months 1-3, 38.40 months 4-24, 48.00 months 25+
Plus all the free oils on the 190PV Level of Essential Rewards Freebies.

Tour of Young Living on 190 PV a month with Essential Rewards

Mini Beauty School=$200.75

Essential Rewards Points Earned 20.08 months 1-3, 40.15 months 4-24, 50.19 months 25+
Plus all the free oils on the 190PV Level of Essential Rewards Freebies.

Tour of Young Living on 190 PV a month with Essential Rewards

Oil Ability

Muscles & Bones=$195.50

Essential Rewards Points Earned 19.55 months 1-3, 39.10 months 4-24, 48.88 months 25+
Plus all the free oils on the 190PV Level of Essential Rewards Freebies.

Tour of Young Living on 190 PV a month with Essential Rewards

Oil Ability

Oils in the Bedroom = $225.75

Essential Rewards Points Earned 22.58 months 1-3, 45.15 months 4-24, 56.44 months 25+
Plus all the free oils on the 190PV Level of Essential Rewards Freebies.

Tour of Young Living on 190 PV a month with Essential Rewards

Oil Ability

Prayer Time=$215.75

Essential Rewards Points Earned 19.20 months 1-3, 38.40 months 4-24, 48.00 months 25+
Plus all the free oils on the 190PV Level of Essential Rewards Freebies.

Tour of Young Living on 190 PV a month with Essential Rewards

Relax=$215.75

Essential Rewards Points Earned 21.58 months 1-3, 43.15 months 4-24, 53.94 months 25+
Plus all the free oils on the 190PV Level of Essential Rewards Freebies.

Tour of Young Living on 190 PV a month with Essential Rewards

Comes with: Melrose, Raven, RC,
DiGize Vitality, EndoFlex Vitality,
Thieves Vitality, and JuvaFlex Vitality

Support Your Immune System=$202.50

Essential Rewards Points Earned 20.25 months 1-3, 40.50 months 4-24, 50.63 months 25+
Plus all the free oils on the 190PV Level of Essential Rewards Freebies.

Tour of Young Living on 300 PV a month with Essential Rewards

Supplements= $321.25

Essential Rewards Points Earned 30.83 months 1-3, 61.65 months 4-24, 77.06 months 25+
Plus all the free oils on the 300PV Level of Essential Rewards Freebies

Tour of Young Living on 300 PV a month with Essential Rewards

Beauty=$309.00

Essential Rewards Points Earned 30.90 months 1-3, 61.80 months 4-24, 77.25 months 25+
Plus all the free oils on the 300PV Level of Essential Rewards Freebies

Tour of Young Living on 300 PV a month with Essential Rewards

Build that Business= $306.75

Essential Rewards Points Earned 30.68 months 1-3, 61.35 months 4-24, 76.69 months 25+
Plus all the free oils on the 300PV Level of Essential Rewards Freebies

Tour of Young Living on 300 PV a month with Essential Rewards

Chef Young Living= $332.75

Essential Rewards Points Earned 30.73 months 1-3, 61.46 months 4-24, 76.84 months 25+
Plus all the free oils on the 300PV Level of Essential Rewards Freebies

Tour of Young Living on 300 PV a month with Essential Rewards

Chef Young Living = $332.75

Essential Rewards Points Earned 30.73
Plus all the free oils on the 300PV Level of Essential Rewards Freebies

Tour of Young Living on 300 PV a month with Essential Rewards

Cleanse those Toxins = $309.75

Essential Rewards Points Earned 30.98 months 1-3, 61.95 months 4-24, 77.44 months 25+
Plus all the free oils on the 300PV Level of Essential Rewards Freebies

Tour of Young Living on 300 PV a month with Essential Rewards

Comes with:
Harmony, Forgiveness, Inner Child,
Present Time, Release, and Valor II

Feel All the Emotions = $312.00

Essential Rewards Points Earned 31.20 months 1-3, 62.40 months 4-24, 78.00 months 25+
Plus all the free oils on the 300PV Level of Essential Rewards Freebies

Tour of Young Living on 300 PV a month with Essential Rewards

Oil Ability

Focus on All the Things= $309.25

Essential Rewards Points Earned 30.93 months 1-3, 61.85 months 4-24, 77.31 months 25+
Plus all the free oils on the 300PV Level of Essential Rewards Freebies

Tour of Young Living on 300 PV a month with Essential Rewards

Oil Ability

Comes with:
Tummygize, SniffleEase, Sleepyize, Owie, GeneYus, and BiteBuster

For the Little Ones= $306.75

Essential Rewards Points Earned 30.68 months 1-3, 61.35 months 4-24, 76.69 months 25+
Plus all the free oils on the 300PV Level of Essential Rewards Freebies

Tour of Young Living on 300 PV a month with Essential Rewards

Oil Ability

Get Cleaning= $301.00

Essential Rewards Points Earned 30.10 months 1-3, 60.20 months 4-24, 75.25 months 25+
Plus all the free oils on the 300PV Level of Essential Rewards Freebies

Tour of Young Living on 300 PV a month with Essential Rewards

Get Rolling and Moving= $316.50

Essential Rewards Points Earned 31.65 months 1-3, 63.30 months 4-24, 79.13 months 25+
Plus all the free oils on the 300PV Level of Essential Rewards Freebies

Tour of Young Living on 300 PV a month with Essential Rewards

Comes with:
Aloes, Cassia, Cedarwood, Cypress, Frankincense, Hyssop, Myrrh, Myrtle, Onycha, and Rose of Sharon.

Oils of Ancient Scripture= $311.00

Essential Rewards Points Earned 31.10 months 1-3, 62.20 months 4-24, 77.75 months 25+
Plus all the free oils on the 300PV Level of Essential Rewards Freebies

Tour of Young Living on 300 PV a month with Essential Rewards

Rock Your Body= $306.75

Essential Rewards Points Earned 30.40 months 1-3, 60.80 months 4-24, 76.00 months 25+
Plus all the free oils on the 300PV Level of Essential Rewards Freebies

APPENDIX C

FOLLOW UP CARDS

Cut out the cards on the other side of the page and place them in a 3x5 index card holder to track your team!

Month 1 Follow-Up

Name_____ Dist# _____

Date _____ Phone _____ Email _____

☆Product User   ☆ Business Builder

❑ If they are a potential business builder to get their oils for free, would they like training? _____
❑ Are they on our team training page? _____
❑ Do they have a copy of the Gameplan book? _____
❑ Do they know how to use the diffuser? _____
❑ Give recipe for respiratory support (10 drops Thieves Vitality, 8 drops Oregano Vitality, 2 drops Frankincense Vitality in a veggie cap as needed); RC in the diffuser, Thieves cough drops as needed, Inner Defense as a supplement for overall immune support, as well as Super C.
❑ Are they on the Oil Ability with Sarah Facebook Page? _____
❑ Invite to class or ask them to host a class. _____
❑ Explain ER, tell them about the promos this month, and how to sign up- tell them you will give them ER ideas via email (mail some of the ER graphics to them from this workbook)
❑ What are the products they want to try? _____

❑ Give them your contact info, an Oily Lifestyle DVD that runs through the kit, and Jordan Schrandt's Welcome Book.

What I mailed or recommended to them:

_____

Month 2 Follow-Up

Name_____Dist# _____

Date _____ Phone _____ Email _____

❑ How are they using their oils?_____
❑ Give them some ideas for pain: Have they tried Cool Azul Pain Cream or the Deep Relief Roll On?

_____

❑ Ask what products they are most interested in: beauty, personal care, cleaning supplies, oils, or supplements. Then give them some ideas based on the essential rewards cards in the Appendix._____
❑ Give them resources: an Oil Ability DVD or CD, a roll on of a new oil they've not tried, or a sample like NingXia or the Thieves cough drops or Thieves laundry soap.
❑ Explain the various reference guides out there.
❑ Tell them about Essential Rewards, email them some different Essential Rewards ideas cards from the Gameplan Workbook Appendix, and explain the promos for the month.

What I mailed or recommended to them:

_____

Month 3 Follow-Up

Name_____Dist# _____

Date _____ Phone _____ Email _____

❑ How are they using their oils?_____
❑ What have they not used?_____
❑ Give them recipe ideas for energy and for relaxing:
   ○ Energy: Super B, NingXia + Nitro, Pure Protein Complete (see the recipe in the Gameplan book for the protein smoothie!), EnRGee oil in the diffuser, or Peppermint.
   ○ Relaxation oils: Stress Away, Tranquil, Peace and Calming 2, Relaxation Massage Oil.
❑ Tell them about Essential Rewards, email them some different Essential Rewards ideas cards from the Gameplan workbook appendix, and explain the promos for the month.

What I mailed or recommended to them:

_____

APPENDIX D

OIL ABILITY RESOURCES TO CATAPULT YOUR TEAM

Did you know that Oil Ability team resources are open to all crossline, upline, and downline members? It's a policy we have kept in place since the very first class. Classes are free and open to all, and training is free and open to all. Why? Because as your team grows, you'll find it harder and harder to fly or drive out of state to train your own team. We'd hope that Young Living leaders across the nation would allow our team members to sit in their classes—because we truly are one big family. If you want ANY of these resources, order them at oilabilityteam.com

So what resources has our team developed? Check them out here.

Facebook. Our team runs a Facebook page thousands strong called "Oil Ability with Sarah" that's updated several times a day with compliant posts. It's a great place to send your leaders and team members for oily education. Pillage the FDA compliant images for your own pages. (Go ahead! We encourage pillaging!) This is about getting oils into every home in the world—if our page helps you out, go for it. Use the material.

Our website. oilabilityteam.com. is where you can pick up DVD's, Gameplan books, Gameplan Bootcamp resources, and audio lectures. We do offer bulk pricing for leaders that want many copies.

WHAT DVD'S HAS SARAH PUT TOGETHER?

Oil Ability 101: the ground up lecture where it all started; centers on the premium starter kit

Oily Lifestyle: the DVD that shows each new member how to use their kit, explains the other items Young Living sells, and how to get on Essential Rewards. It's a must-have DVD for follow up for any business builder. 30 minutes.

Scavenger Hunt: a hilarious 4-minute icebreaker video for your classes featuring Sarah's 5 kids, showing off what an oil-infused lifestyle looks like. This breaks up your lecture and introduces your audience to a personal tour of a chemical-free home. This video has gotten rave reviews and is a tremendous asset to your teaching!! 3 minutes.

Why Do Young Living As A Business: This little ditty is what helped grow our team to 800 sellers in 18 months. I chase all 101 classes with this. 15 minutes.

Business DVD's:

FDA Compliance Training: A full 30-minute compliance training for those that truly don't want to lose their business. Learn the right speech. 30 minutes.

How to Fill Classes without Knowing People: Our tips on filling classes, no matter where you live! 20 minutes

WHAT CD'S HAS SARAH PUT TOGETHER?

Essential Oils 101. 45 minutes, this is an extremely powerful tool for busy potential oilers to listen to in the car. It's been called the best tool, save Gameplan, that the team has put together.

Gameplan. (You read that correctly. The Gameplan book is now available as an audio CD for your leaders to train in the car!)

WHAT BOOKS HAS SARAH WRITTEN?

Gameplan: A Comprehensive Strategy Guide to go from starter kit to Silver

Gameplan The Workbook: This is a companion workbook that makes the book come alive for your team. It puts action to your dreams and goals. This isn't a fill-in-the-blank workbook. It helps you lay out serious goals chapter by chapter.

(Coming Soon) **Gameplan 2**: a powerful book for Silvers and above—your entire strategy must change!

(Coming Soon) **Silver Bootcamp Gameplan Style** a 5-week guided boot-camp. Let Sarah train your leaders in small group format. Also for personal use!

Find all of this at oilabilityteam.com